Turtle Creek Chorale (*deceased in italic*): John S. Acker - Mace Adams - Scott Adams - Carolyn Ade... Anne Albritton - Brian Alden - David Alexander - G. Bradley Alford - *Rick Alford* - Brian Allen - G. Clayton All... - Skip Allen - Stephen D. Allen - David Allison - Frances Almanzo - Hector Alvarado - Michae... - Judith Anderson - Peter Marshall Anderson - Wayne Anderson - Gregg Andrews - *Rick And*... - Dale Arant - Keith Arcement - Darren Armstrong - Debbie Armstrong - Steve Arnn - Rudy Arrendo... has - Jeff Atkins - Marc Atkinson - Kenneth Atterhout - Garrison Ausbum - Matt Austin - Mike Autry - Tricia Avery - Bill (Bob) Bailey - *Keith Bailey* - Michael A. Baird - Richard Baird - Daryl Baker - Jeffrey Joe Baker - Mary Lou Baker - *Milton M. Baker* - Ken Bales - Marta F. Balleste - Tony Balquin - Daryl Banks - *James (Buddy) Barkalow* - Phil Barnett - Ernest Barrens - *William (Bill) Patrick Barry* - Buddy Bartley - Ruben Basantes - Randol Alan (Randy) Bass - Sam Bass - *David Bassett* - Rodney Bateman - David Bates - David E. Bates - Johnny Bauman - Terry Baxter - Thomas S. Bayer, Jr. - Steven Bayes - Mark Beach - John Beall - *Dean Beasley* - Michael Becerra - John Benham - Joe Lynwood Bennett - Cheryl Berman - Patrick Betasso - Ralph Beulls - Anthony Binard - *Bill Binns* - Chuck Bischoff - Tom Bizette - A. G. Black - Ralph Blackburn - Wallace Blair - Roderick E. Blake - J. Pat Blanchard-Modisette - Tim Blanchard-Modisette - Lynn Blankenship - Randy Blankenship - Carlton D. Blanton - Mike Bledsoe - Wayne (Sam) Blehm - Brett Bleuer - Jonathan Blevins - Tony Blowers - Fred Blue - Clarence (Sam) Blumenshine - Quinn Boardman - Dennis Boatright - Randy Boatright - Ron Bobbitt - Lance Boltz - *Tom Bonifanti* - Frank Bonner, II - Reid Bonner - Billy Boone - Gary Born - Michael Borschert - Billy B. Boughton - Gerald Box - Anthony (Tony) Boyd - Blake Boyd - Michael Boyd - Tab Boyles - Ella Mae Boyles-Payton - Kirk Bradford - Michael Bradley - *Richard Brado* - Henry Branstetter - Michael Brantley - Joey Brashier - Kurtis Braxton - John P. Bray - Becca Brese - Dennis Brickman - Christopher Bride - *Emerson Briney* - Greg Britt - Tony Britt - J. David Brock - Steve Brock - Bryan A. Brooks - Patrick Brotherton - *Benn Brown* - Carlas Brown - Darin Brown - Glenn Brown - James Brown - Mark Brown - *Don Bryant* - Blaine Buchenau - Connie Buchholz - Jamie Buck - Jeff (Danny) Buck - C.E. Bunkley, III - Jack Bunning - David Burbee - Brian Burcham - Paul A. Burdett - Steve Burgos - Jonathan Burnett - Adam Burns - Tom Burns - Sherry Burnside - Mark Burton - *Michael Burton* - Patrick Burton - Carl Busbey - Jack Busby - Harry Bushnell - John (Bohn) Butler - Tom Button - Jack Buzbee - Bill Byas - Chris Byers - *Jay Caddell* - Michael Cain - Dan Calhoun - Chris Camp - Robert Campbell - Craig Canant - Tom Caraway - Elijah Cardona - Christopher Carfanio - Mark Cargill - Larry Carmicheal - Rob Carpenter - Steve Carpenter - Michael Carrillo - John Carroll - Albert Carter - Bruce Carter - Jim Carter - Larry Carter - Ron Carter - Donald Caruso - Charles Cason III - Marc Cassentini - Wayne Cavender - Eddie Cavin - Scott Cecil - Bradley Chamberlain - Jim Chambers - T. Michael Chandler - David Cheek - Jamey Cheek - *Ben Cherry* - Bill Chown - Matt Christensen - Stan Christensen - Justin Christenson - Clayton Clark - Dennis Clark - Dwayne Clark - Frank Clark - Bill Cleaveland - Darryl Clement - Howard Clement - Robert (Bob) Clement - Douglas (Doug) Clifton - Mike Cline - John Clizbe - Kent Cochran - Harry Coddington - Art Cole - Michael Cole - Robert Cole - James Coley - Jeremy Collette - Douglas Collins - Phillip Collins - Larry Colyar - John Connell - Alvin I. Cooper, Jr. - Lee Corbin - Richard Cordray - Greg Cotton - Tim Cowan - *Bret Cox* - Cece Cox - Garry Cox - Grady Coyle - Michael Crawford - Fred Crescente - Wade Creson - Justin Cris-Tensen - Glenn F. Cron - Ron Crouch - Joel Cruz - Richard Cruz - Randy Culbreth - Todd Cunningham - Steve Currey - Daryl Curry - Paul Curry - Richard Curtin - Collin Curtis - John Czerwonka - Joey DaGuerre - David Daigle - Mike Dalessandro - Daniel DalPoas - *Dale Damon* - Melvin Damvillier - *David Daniel* - Herbert H (Bret) Daniel - Art Darnold - Edward F. Darr II - Keith Davenport - Doug Davidson - Mykel (Michael) Davidson - Scott Davidson - C. Jackson Davis - Doug Davis - Jerry Davis - *John Davis* - Mark Davis - Mike Davis - Rob Davis - *Tom Davis* - Wayne L. Davis - Danny de la Rosa - Cubby Dean - *Ron Dean* - Dan Deason - Erwin DeBord - Harry DeBorde - Jim Dees - Joe Demourelle - David Dempsey - Eddie Dennis - Chuck Denny - Rick Dent - Raun DeVries - Thomas DeWitte - David W. Dick - Ron Dickenson - Damon Didawick - Mike Dilbeck - Bob Dillard - Ken Dilleland - Chad Dingman - Allyn Dixon - Dan Dixon - Patrick Dixon - Terry Dobson - Cole Dodson - Steve Dolloff - Gene Dolphus - Ashley Donde - Matt Dorf - Cynthia Dorn-Navarette - Darren Dorsey - Brandon Doubek - Michael Doughman - Bruce Douglas - Richard E. Dowdy - Ed Dowgiallo - Timothy J. Dowler - Allen Drexel - Elvira Dreyfus - Nicole Dreyfus - *Brian Drummond* - John Duarte - Terry Duffield - *Dick DuFore* - Randy Duits - Daniel (Dan) Duke - *Terry Duke* - Robert Dulaney - *Tracy Duncan* - Davie Duque - Don Dureau - Cedric Durham - Bruce Easley - Dale Eckler, Jr. - R. Maurice Edens

- Skip Edmonds - Chan Edmondson - Dan Edwards - *Rodney Edwards* - Shay Edwards - John Eger - Bruce Ehrhardt - Tom Eichenberger - John Eldridge - Tim Elhard - Ted Elinor - Patrick Ellender - Lyle A Ellerback - David Elliott - Edwin Ellis - Ward Elmendorf - Greg Emery - Robert Emery - Jim Enright - Jeff Ensign - Jim Erickson - Elizabeth Espersen - Ernesto R. Espinolola - Don Essmiller - *Darrin Etheridge* - Randall Etherton - *Robert H. Euler* - Gary Evans - *James Evans* - Michael L Evans, Ph.D. - Peggy Everson - David Fahnie - Brad Faidley - James Farmer - Tim Farmer - Tom Faucett - Rod Faulkner - Denny Favor - Jonathan Fears - James Feaster - Billy Ferguson - Bruce Ferko - Rod Ferrara - James Fesalbon - David Fessenden - J. Lyle Fields - Randy Fikes - Louis Fincher - F. Earl Fitzsimmons - Chet Flake - Ed Flaspoehler - David Fleming - Dr. Richard L. Fleming - Tim Flemmons - Bruce Flint - Jullian Flores - Glen Floyd - Rick Fogerty - Chris Foley - Stephen (Steve) Folse - *David T. Ford* - Mark Ford - Randy Ford - William Ford - Chris Forman - Jay Forte - Scott Foster - *Wayne A. Foster* - Tom Fowler - Drew Frailey - Douglas R. Frankel - Randy Franklin - Jim Frederick - Michael Frederick - *Steve Freeman* - Will Freeman - Stephen Frels - Charles Fruth - Bill Fry - Ron Fuller - William Paul Futrell - *Trent Gagnon* - John Gallaher - Graham F. Gallais - Floyd Galvan - Richard Galvan - George Gammon - Gil Garcia - Hector Garcia - J. Guadelupe Garcia - John F. Garcia - Steve Garcia - John (Jay) Gardner - Neal L. Gardner - Patrick Gardner - Landon Garrett - Kenneth W. Gartman - Bernardo Garza - Joe Garza - Robert Garza - Lucas S. Gavitt - Sean Gawel - Martin Owen Gemoets - Charlie Gentry - David Gentry - *Phil Gerber* - Chuck Gibson - Owen Gibson - *Thom Gibson* - David Giersch - Jeffrey Giles - Ken Gilleland - George Gillispie - Darrell Gipson - Michael Gissler - Don Glover - Alan Scott Goeringer - Stan Goff - Ryan Golze - Anthony E. Gonzales - Ed Gonzales - *Ralph T. Gonzales* - Greg Gonzalez - Camille Goode - Mark Goodheart - Ford Goodlove - Johnny Goolsby - Susan Gore - Tony Gore - Seth Gowans - *Miguel Graham* - Jack Gramlich - Stan Graner - Mike Grant - Adam Graves - Bradley Graves - *Kevin Gray* - Wayne Gray - Brian Green - *Mike Green* - Larry Greene - Thomas (Tom) Greene - Craig Gregory - David Grelle - Keith Griffin - Maurice Griffin - Christian Griffith - Peter Grimmett - Curtis Grisham - David Grogg - Chris Gross - Barry (Rob) Grzesiak - James Gudat - Debbie Guerra - Martin Guerra - Victor Guerrero, III - Larry Guest - Joshua Gutierrez - Richard G. Guy - Rob Guy - Samuel Gwin - Vincent (Vince) Hackett, Jr. - Howard Haile - *Alan Hajek* - Bly Halbrook - Joseph Haley - Dale Hall Doug Hall - Rick Hall - Kathy Haltom - Dean Hamilton - Steve Hammond - Rusty Hampton - Mark Hamrick - Sylvan Garret Hancock - Dwain Handley - Harley Handy - Will Handy - Mark Haneke - Douglas Hannan - *Kirk Hansen* - Baer Hanusz-Rajkowski - Dean Harberts - Patrick Harden - Michael Hardin - David Hardt - Brian Harkins - David Harp - James S. Harp, III - *Charles A. (Chuck) Harper* - Dale Harris - Gene Harris - Mark W. Harris - Stewart Harris - Derek Harrison - Thomas Hartley - Kevin Hasson - Jim Haun - Mark E. Hawkins - Mark Hawkins - *Mike Hearn* - Bill K. J.. Hebert - Steve Heckman - Steven Hefner - William Ross Heidmann - Troy Heine - Bob Helm - Douglas Helms - Gene Hempy - Johnny Henderson - John M. Henrikson - David Henry - *Cornell Henson* - George Henson - William J. Herm - *Bill Herod* - Ivan Herrera - Michael R. Herrington - Phil Herrington - Chris Heslep - Richard S. (Rick) Hetherly - Clayton Hiatt - *Allen Hicks* - Jim High - Danny Hill - Shane Edward Hill - Dingo Hines - James Hing - *Jeff Hinkle-Dubois* - Kevin Hodges - Charles Hodnett - Greg Hoeft - Jeremy Hoekstra - Keith A. Hoffman - Reed R. Hoke - J. B. Holman - Daniel Holquin - Mark Hoover - Julian Hores - Timothy Horman - John Hornay - John Hornecker - David Houston - David Howard - Joey Howard - W. Allen Howard - Janet Howe - Mark Howell - Mickey S. Howell - Rick Howell - *Bill Howie* - Tyrone Howze - Gerald Huber - Luke Huddleston - Justin Hughes - T. Ray Humphrey - Jerry Humphreys - Robert Huneke - George Hunter - Scott H. Hunter - Bob Hurley - Navaid Hussain - Ryan Hutchinson - John Hyink - *Don Hylin* - Myron Ice - Blaine Ichimura - Scott Igo - William Igo - *Tim Ihloff* - Joel Ihms - William Irwin - Gregory C. Isenberg - *Bill Jackson* - Floyd L. Jackson - Foy Jackson - James P. Jackson - Daniel Jacob - George (Jake) Jacobs - Thomas Jaekels - Bill Jagoe - J. Jack Jakubowski - Tino Jalomo - Coy Dell James - Ric James - Bruce Jaster - Phyllis Jeff - David Jenkins - *Joel Jenner* - Stan Jensen - Scott Jeppeson - Bob Jerger - Robin Jesseman - Jim John - Bret Johnson - Don Johnson - Forrest Johnson - Fred Johnson - Jimmy Johnson - Rick Johnson - Bill Johnston - David L. Johnston - Jeff Johnston - Ben Joiner - Steven Jolly - Don Jones - Gabriel Tim Jones - John G. Jones - Judith Jones - Karen S. Jones - Ricky Jones - David Jordan - James (Jim) Jordan - Scott Jordan - Travis Jordan - Kenneth Jorns - Earl Joyner - Ibis Kaba - Jeffrey Kanters - Ted Karpf - Bobby Kates - Michael Kaufman - Steven Kays - Kit Kayton - John Kazee - Adam Keim - J. R. Keith - Louis Kelly - Ella Kendrick - Don Kennedy - Scott Kennedy - Steven Elkins Kennedy - Wes Kennedy - Ronald (Ron) Kercenneck - *Dwight Kilgore* - Jack Kille - Dawayne Kimery - Jason D. Kimmell - Michael Kimmons - Charles King - Rhett King - Chip Kizziar - Chris Klecker - *Kent Klein* - Christopher Kleker - Ray Knapp - Terry Knapp - Bud Knight - Mark Knight - Mecia Knott - James Kondysar - Michael Konow - Bill Kotch - Trent Kotch - Chris Kouvelis, Jr. - Joe Kunkel - Steven Kuntz - Tom Kunze - Keith Kuykendall - Tony Kuzmanich - Rick Kyle - Mike Lalonde - John L. Lambert - Michael Lambert - Sharon Lammers - Darryl Lancing - David Land -

Introduction

"Breathe!" was chosen as the title of this book primarily because of the poem which follows, written to acknowledge a transformation Jason Walker experienced when he joined the Turtle Creek Chorale (after hesitating for almost five years). It was also meant to sound like something a conductor might say to his singers to make sure they have enough energy to sustain a long phrase. Readers, then, are being exhorted to enter the world of the Chorale without holding back, so that putting this book away will be a little like leaving the Morton H. Meyerson Symphony Center after a concert, with the words and music and images of the Chorale still fresh in their minds.

This book may be a breath of fresh air for some, but it isn't aimed at anyone in particular. There are fresh things to learn about the Turtles as performers…The way they blend is amazing since their voices vary tremendously in quality. Nearly all are gay, though they come from every walk of life and have many different interests away from the Chorale (and like different music). They work together and laugh together harmoniously—the best of brothers, sharing what they feel. The way they encourage and help each other carries over to the children and should be noted by those who haven't made up their minds about same-sex marriage.

At a time when conformity of thought is being celebrated in a way that many of us find suffocating, the Turtles celebrate openness, and not only when they're singing. In expressing their emotions and opinions, anything goes. They feel safe when they are together, and often refer to the Sammons Center for the Arts, where they rehearse, as "the only place where it's completely okay to be myself." Yet they are not a family because of place, and healthy families are never unanimous in matters of opinion. What unites them is the sense that the same bedrock is underlying all their lives, a quiet confidence that comes from self-knowledge. At one point they stopped fighting themselves and began to take stock of everything they had to give. What stays in the mind after visiting with them, or observing them at a rehearsal, is the way they create their songs, conduct their business and express their feelings without ulterior motives. They've become so focused on giving, as opposed to having, that they are giving things they didn't know they had. "My time with you," during which members make a measured contribution of talent and energy, has become "our time together," a time of creative exaltation where the certain thing is not what will happen, but the joy of discovery when it does.

This book has been written to celebrate twenty-five years of laughing at each other and with each other—listening to each other, learning from each other—of living with each other as members of a family. There are elements of church, elements of school, elements of the workplace, though the singing is never just a job. Something that happens when these men come together to sing bears on their identity, changes their lives, and has the potential to change ours.

In the spirit of the Chorale, it's not important to define what the Chorale is because that violates the spirit of openness that allows the Chorale to grow and change in response to its own needs and the community's. Rather, this book will attempt to show the Chorale in action. The text will attempt to describe what the men do, and why, and how; the pictures will show what they look like, how they behave, how they have fun; the compact disc reproduces their music. Let the reader form his or her own idea of what is going on. As for the men, the meaning of the Chorale to them isn't always the same. They are unanimous about only one thing: they love to sing.

I BREATHED AGAIN!

AUDIO TRACK NUMBER ONE

I was a strange little boy, constantly afraid.
Always running to hide and never running to play.
I was scared of everything.
I was scared of the day and scared of the night.
I was scared of the dark and scared of the light.
I would lie in my bed curled up, eyes closed,
Afraid to take a breath, and I would think to myself,
"Is it ok to breathe? No, not yet."

I grew to be a young man, but the fear never went away.
Though I got pretty good at knowing just what to say
To make people think everything was "OK."
But, the fear was always there, my constant companion.
Fear of life and of death and most of all being abandoned
And left alone in my bed, curled up, eyes closed,
Afraid to take a breath, and I would think to myself,
"Is it ok to breathe? No, not yet."

So, I decided one day to make the fear go away.
I would deny what was the truth and call it a lie.
Men are supposed to love women, not other men.
And the fear looked me in the face and laughed and said,
"I win again!"

All these years have gone by and I'm blue in the face
From holding my breath while running this race called LIFE.
Always looking behind, never looking ahead.
God, how I wish I were that little boy in bed,
Curled up, eyes closed,
Afraid to take a breath, and I would think to myself,
"Is it ok to breathe? No, not yet."

Where does this road go?
Where does this story end?
Oddly enough, right where it began.
Only this time instead of fear that little boy is filled with a song
Because he's found his family and knows where he belongs.
And, this morning…

I breathed again.

I Breathed Again!
by Jason Walker

with music from
Reflections
Songs Without Words
by Danny Ray

Twenty-five years of making music and changing lives: the premier concert (June, 1980) presented by the newly formed Turtle Creek Chorale (inset photo). The Chorale, 2004, adopting the theme "Imagine A World Where Everyone Focused On Harmony Rather Than Their Differences."

Breathe!

25 YEARS WITH THE TURTLE CREEK CHORALE

In loving memory of Ann Davidson

Dr. Timothy Seelig - Turtle Creek Chorale   *Artistic Director*
Jeff Putnam - Avenue Publishers, Inc., Dallas, Texas   *Publisher & Writer*
Joseph Rattan - Joseph Rattan Design, Dallas, Texas   *Design, Layout & Illustration*

With appreciation to all of the Turtle Creek Chorale members who shared their thoughts, memories and pictures. And special thanks to Shawn Northcutt, Shawn Northcutt Photography, for his beautiful photographic work.

TURTLE CREEK CHORALE

1980 ⋈ 2005
25 YEARS OF HARMONY

BREATHE!   25 YEARS WITH THE TURTLE CREEK CHORALE

Copyright ©2004 by Jeff Putnam and Joseph Rattan

Avenue Publishers, Inc., 4038 Lemmon Ave., Suite 101, Dallas, Texas 75219

All rights reserved. No portion of this publication may be reproduced or transmitted in any form or by any means, including mechanical, audio, or electronic, or any information storage and retrieval system known or to be invented, without permission granted in writing by the publisher.

Library of Congress Cataloging-in-Publication Data
Putnam, Jeff.
Breathe! : 25 years with the Turtle Creek Chorale :
Artistic Director, Dr. Timothy Seelig / design and illustration, Joseph Rattan ; text, Jeff Putnam.
     p. cm.
ISBN 0-9761661-0-0 (alk. paper)
 1. Turtle Creek Chorale. 2. Seelig, Timothy. I. Rattan, Joseph, 1958-
II. Title.

ML28.D35T84 2004
782.8'06'07642812--dc22

2004021124

Manufactured in the United States of America
First Printing, 2004

photo: Shawn Northcutt

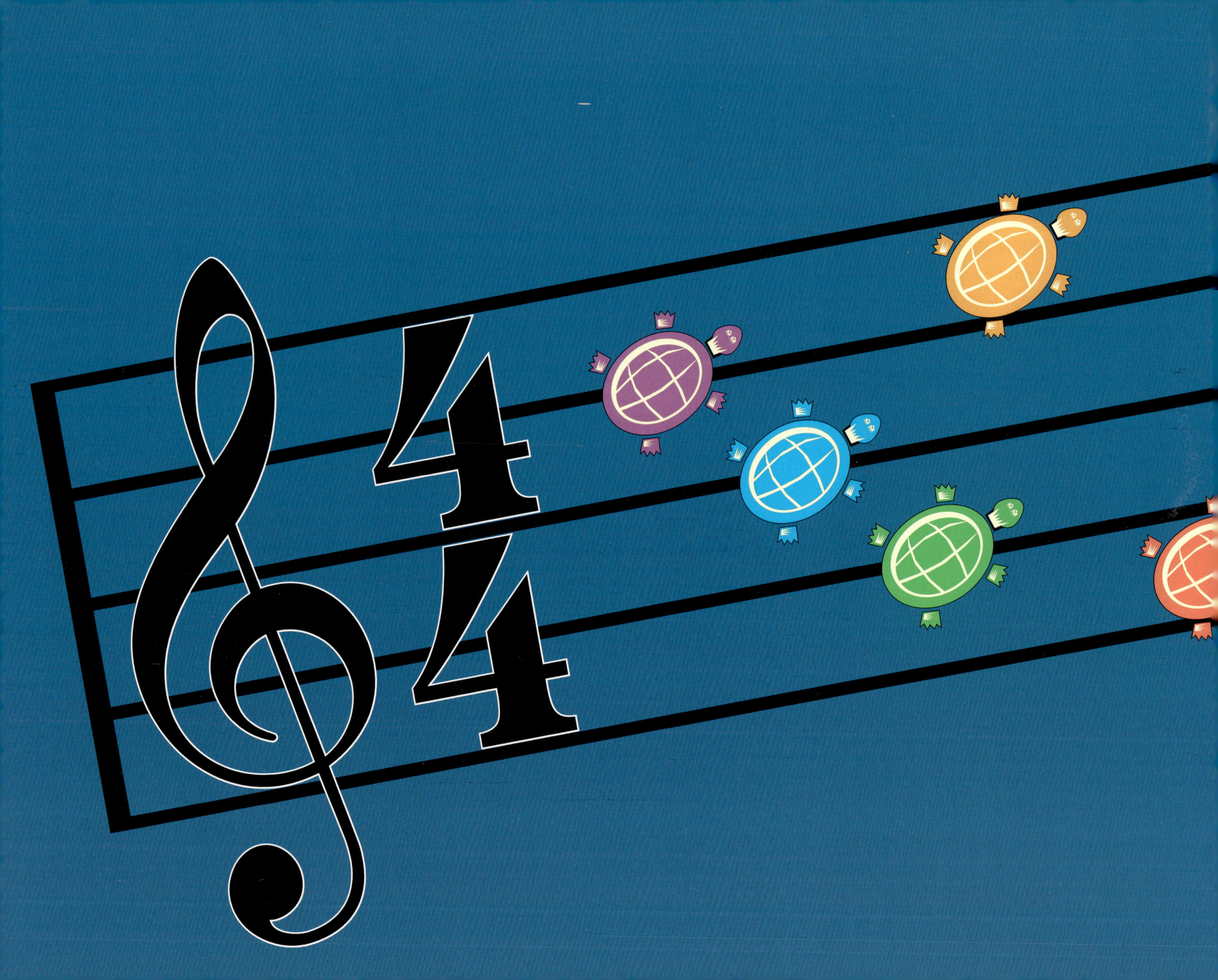

AUDIO TRACK NUMBER TWO

Making

MUSIC AND CHANGING LIVES

I dreamed a dream. I dreamed a dream.
I dreamed a dream, a silent dream of a land not faraway.
Where no bird sang, no steeples rang and teardrops fell like rain.
I dreamed a dream, a silent dream, a silent dream of a land so filled with pride.
That every song, both weak and strong withered and died.
I dreamed a dream. No alleluia, not one hosanna, no song of love, no lullaby.
And no choir sang to change the world. No pipers played; no dancers twirled.
I dreamed a dream, a silent dream. Silent, silent.

Awake, awake, awake. Awake, awake my soul and sing.
The time for praise has come. The silence of the night has passed,
A new day has begun. Let music never die in me. Forever let my spirit sing.
Wherever emptiness is found, let there be joy and glorious sound.
Let music never die in me. Forever let my spirit sing.
Let all our voices join as one to praise the Giver of the song.
Awake, awake.
Let music live. Let music live.

The Awakening
music & lyrics: Joseph M. Martin

illustration: Joseph Rattan

MAKING MUSIC AND CHANGING LIVES

The members of the TCC are attracted to the chorus by its music. Once there, they realize it is so much more than just a chorus. The music-making takes them to different cities, foreign countries and places within their own city they never dreamed they might be, singing music they never dreamed they would sing, from Strauss to Soul Sisters.

Suppose you've just heard that there's a group of amateur musicians in town, 225 voices strong, and their publicity says you're about to hear something "like no other sound on earth." Might you not go to your first concert tongue in cheek, wondering if you were about to hear a sound that would wake the dead? (And if you were once such a cynical soul, what a surprise.) But it's a rare person who hasn't heard good things about the Turtles by word of mouth or read something in the paper or heard a CD or heard the Chorale during *After Goodbye*, the Emmy award-winning documentary. And of course the Chorale has its fans who try to take in as many concerts as they can. The sound of the Chorale really is like no other sound, you will be forced to admit, and they aren't trying to back up a boast: the Chorale is consciously going its own way.

An audition for the Chorale is like no other audition on earth, at least in retrospect, because voices aren't selected on the basis of training, power, or even beauty. Of course these qualities count for something, but none is as important as a love of singing, a sound that freely expresses the singer's feelings, mapping his "inscape." (A professional, "made" sound may well satisfy commercial and artistic expectations, but we're not able to tell what the singer is really feeling.) Nor are voices selected for their ability to blend. Neither the straight-tone English school nor the operatic voice is required. These singers have a sympathetic resonance with one another and what makes them one is a harmony in what they're feeling and not a uniform way of doing something with muscles in their throats.

Blend is achieved by keeping each voice within what artistic director Dr. Timothy Seelig calls "the beauty box." Voices will differ in size, color, timbre, etc., but it's important for each singer to know the parameters within which his voice communicates feelings most pleasingly.

In rehearsals, members learn to respect parameters of feeling, also. They can pour out their souls, yes, but they're not supposed to lose themselves in the outpouring. Something is retained of who they are, of who Dr. Seelig is, something customary. T. Michael Chandler tells what it feels like:

"A huge part of bringing this music down to message-making is Tim. There's a process he goes through. Rehearsing the words or notes we get to the point that all the emotions are bailed out. Then he brings us back and says: go to that point and don't let it go any further." But how? "You look into his eyes, and follow his hands, and you find yourself at home, which is a place of trust. So then you and the music don't matter any more. In

Antoine Spencer has been Principal or Assistant Accompanist for the Chorale since August, 1991. His mastery at the keyboard enhances the Chorale's sound in every style of music. Audiences everywhere give him ovations; he is a TCC treasure. Here he is assisted by singer Wayne Taylor.

The most recorded male chorus in the world. The Turtle Creek Chorale has over thirty recordings to its credit.

The singers prepare for their six performances in Montreal, 2004, at the Gay and Lesbian Association of Choruses International Festival, *Vive la Musique.*

The boys warm up in the beauty of Denver's summer sun for the International GALA festival, 1992.

other words, all your homework is done, you know the music and the words and you find yourself at home." "Home" here is both an intimate and a commodious place, because for a few moments during the concert it's a place where all of us belong, performers and audience alike.

Rusty Allen describes the same phenomenon by likening Tim Seelig to a prism, an image that evokes the lightning rapidity with which the conductor asks for sounds, weaves them together and flicks them to the audience.

"There's an emotional line we do not cross in performance. We go to the line but do not cross. We focus everything on him: he's the prism that puts it out… As a chorus, we always 'put it out there.' As Tim has said, 'bless it, release it: let it go.' Because I've learned there are coincidences. One must leave one's heart open musically, spiritually, and lovingly, for the good things to come back to us. And they do come to us, over and over again. What greater gift can one receive? I think this is the very core of what it has meant to me to be in the Chorale."

What comes back to the Chorale from the audience is more than applause. The audience is answering the openness of the Chorale with an openness of its own. Emotions are wakened everywhere, and we're seeing each other through tears—there's a fun-house tilt as we glance down the rows. People are brought together this way sometimes in emergencies: there's a sense that we've all taken part in something extraordinary, something completely unexpected—even those who, after all the rehearsals, know every note. The Turtles have been taught that if they give 100 percent, the audience will respond in kind, while 99 percent or anything less will fail to engage them, and they won't be moved as much as they could be.

The perfection, the degree of polish can seem magical, but this doesn't feel like a crowd of perfectionists luxuriating in their mastery of tiny details. If they seem to have surprised themselves, they probably have. There's no question that they did in Montreal. Kirk Bradford and Rob Nichols recall what happened.

Kirk: "We paid for an extra two hour rehearsal because we were insecure about our repertoire. We'd gone up there with big doubts. Some of these other groups had unbelievable resources and here we were with a piano, a trumpet and a flute. After the final a cappella piece, "Serenade of Life," we didn't know till we'd finished the last note…There were two seconds of silence that seemed like an eternity…Then the audience jumped to their feet and we realized they got it, and at the same time we did, too. The circle-of-lives thing: what we were going to be when we grew up. We didn't meet our dreams, but this is what we did do. The most amazing thing that happened was that Tim didn't cut off the last fortissimo note as he normally would. His hands went down to his side and we sang the crescendo as one voice, cutting off 140 singers with the slightest nod of his head. Had we not all been unified or connected with him at that moment it wouldn't have worked. After that no one would say that what was selected wasn't right for us."

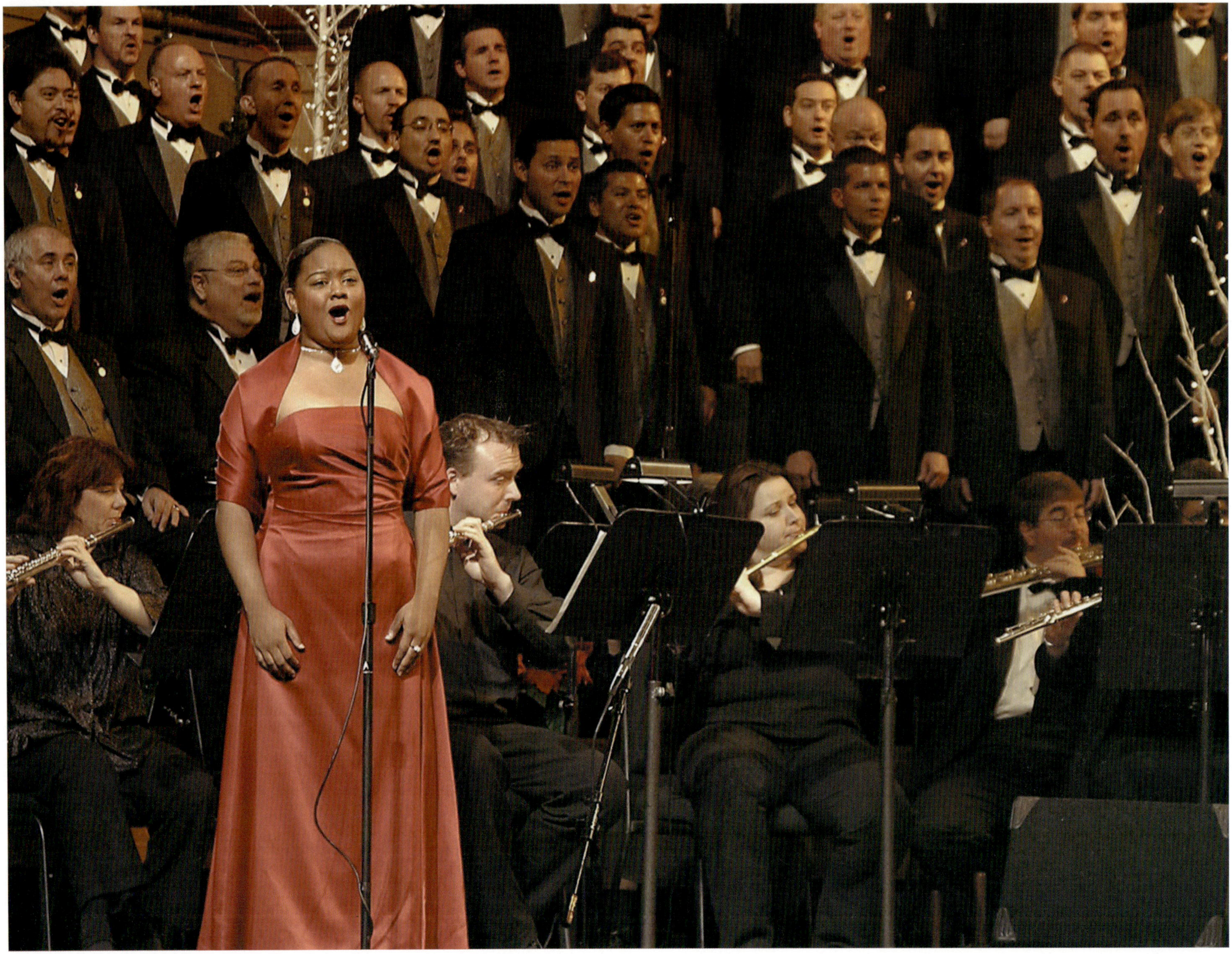

Rob: "It was one of the two greatest moments in my life, and both came to me through the Chorale. The first was some years ago after 'Star-gazing,' when I was alone watching a meteor shower. Thoughts came to me through the music that helped me change my life. But what happened in Montreal when we were finishing the piece…" He composes himself. "Leading up to it we were standing in rows for five minutes, maybe—an eternity. I was meditating, thinking how glad I was to be there. Backstage, in rehearsal the day before, I think I'd finally got the impact of the piece. But when I was about to go on I was afraid I was going to lose it. It all came to me in those moments at the end of the piece, my connection to Tim, standing there with his hands at his side; my appreciation of the audience. I started crying as soon as we got offstage…Now it's a 'musical scar'… I'll always remember how I felt at that moment and all kinds of things trigger the memory…"

No doubt many in the audience are similarly scarred for life.

Small groups allow the chorale to perform more than 50 appearances per year for a wide array of worthy causes. Here are three of those groups (clockwise from left): Chamber Chorus, Turtle Soup and ENCORE!

Collaboration with other artists through the years has become a hallmark of the TCC, from the Dallas Symphony Orchestra to the Dallas Opera. Here, the 12 flutes of Flutes Unlimited accompany, with soprano Tiffany Roberts.

13

● AUDIO TRACK NUMBER THREE

Again, again we come and go, changing.
Hands join, unjoin in love and fear,
 grief and joy.
The circles turn, each giving into each, into all
Only music keeps us here,
 only music keeps us here,
Each by all the others held.
In the hold of hands and eyes we turn in pairs
That joining, joining each to all again.
And then we turn aside, alone
Out of the sunlight gone
Into the darker circles of return.

Within the circles of our lives
We dance the circles of the years
The circle of the seasons within the
 circles of the years
The cycles of the moon within the
 circles of the seasons,
The circles of our reasons
Within the cycles of the moon.

The Circles of our Lives
music: David Brunner
lyrics: Wendell Berry

Again, again we come and go changed, changing.
Hands join, unjoin in love and fear,
 grief and joy.
The circles turn, each giving into each, into all
Only music keeps us here,
 only music keeps us here,
Each by all the others held
In the hold of hands and eyes we turn in pairs
That joining, joining each to all again.
And then we turn aside,
And then we turn alone
Out of the sunlight gone
Into the darker circles of return
Within the circles of our lives
We dance the circle of the years
Within the circle of our lives
We dance the circles of the years,
(Within the circle of our lives)
Within the circle of our lives.

Within the circles of our lives.

The circles of the lives of the TCC have included treasured people who have passed on, such as Assistant Conductor and Composer Kris Anthony (left) and Randy Rhea (right), long time PR representative and singer. Both of these wonderful men were profiled in *After Goodbye: An AIDS Story* on PBS. Longtime accompanist, arranger and "Mom" Anne Albritton has been a huge part of our family circle. She is pictured here with her partner, Trigger.

14

Making music for the Chorale at times has meant using more than our voices, as pictured left.

Small pictures (clockwise from top right): The Women's Chorus of Dallas performs its breathtaking "Adiemus" at the GALA festival in Montreal, 2004; During the Chorale's 1995 tour to Europe, the first nationally recognized AIDS benefit was proudly performed in the beautiful Rudolfinum in Prague; TCC in June of 1980.

In less than an hour, the concert had turned around who knows how many years of hatred....

I had a very prim and proper elderly lady sitting to my left by herself. Just moments before the concert began, the lady leaned over and whispered softly to me, "Did you know that most of the gentlemen in this choir are queer?" I looked at her very matter of factly and simply stated, "Yes, I do know that. My lover and I are both members." Well...you would have thought she had seen a ghost! She very gingerly scooted to the left, as far as she could lean without having to actually move. I could see her watching me with this odd look on her face, that I could honestly say was mortal fear, for she was sitting next to me, the queer. But as the evening progressed, she leaned more and more to the middle. And finally, by the last song, she was weeping and holding my hand.... After the concert we stood, and she turned and gave me the largest hug her small body could muster. She leaned into my ear and said the most amazing words: "I am so sorry." "About what?" was my honest reply. "For my hatred all my life towards gay people. Thank you for mending my heart," she replied. We just stood there hugging and crying with each other. I was stunned! In less than an hour, the concert had turned around who knows how many years of hatred or misunderstanding, and torn down one more wall. It was definitely a life-changing moment for me!

from a letter to Tim Seelig
from a new chorale member

One of the most exciting and prestigious invitations for any chorus is to perform at an American Choral Directors Association convention. The TCC is honored to have auditioned for—and to have been invited to—eight such conventions: 2 state, 3 regional and 3 national. Pictured here is the chorus at the national convention in San Diego, 1997. These conventions give the chorale an opportunity to hone its art to the highest possible level and perform for thousands of choral directors and other choral singers. It is without a doubt the chorus's most nerve-racking experience—and we keep auditioning to do it again. (Go figure.)
Composer Robert Seeley (right) and his partner, lyricist Robert Espindola, sit in the Meyerson for a rehearsal of some of the brilliant music they have created as sung by the TCC.

17

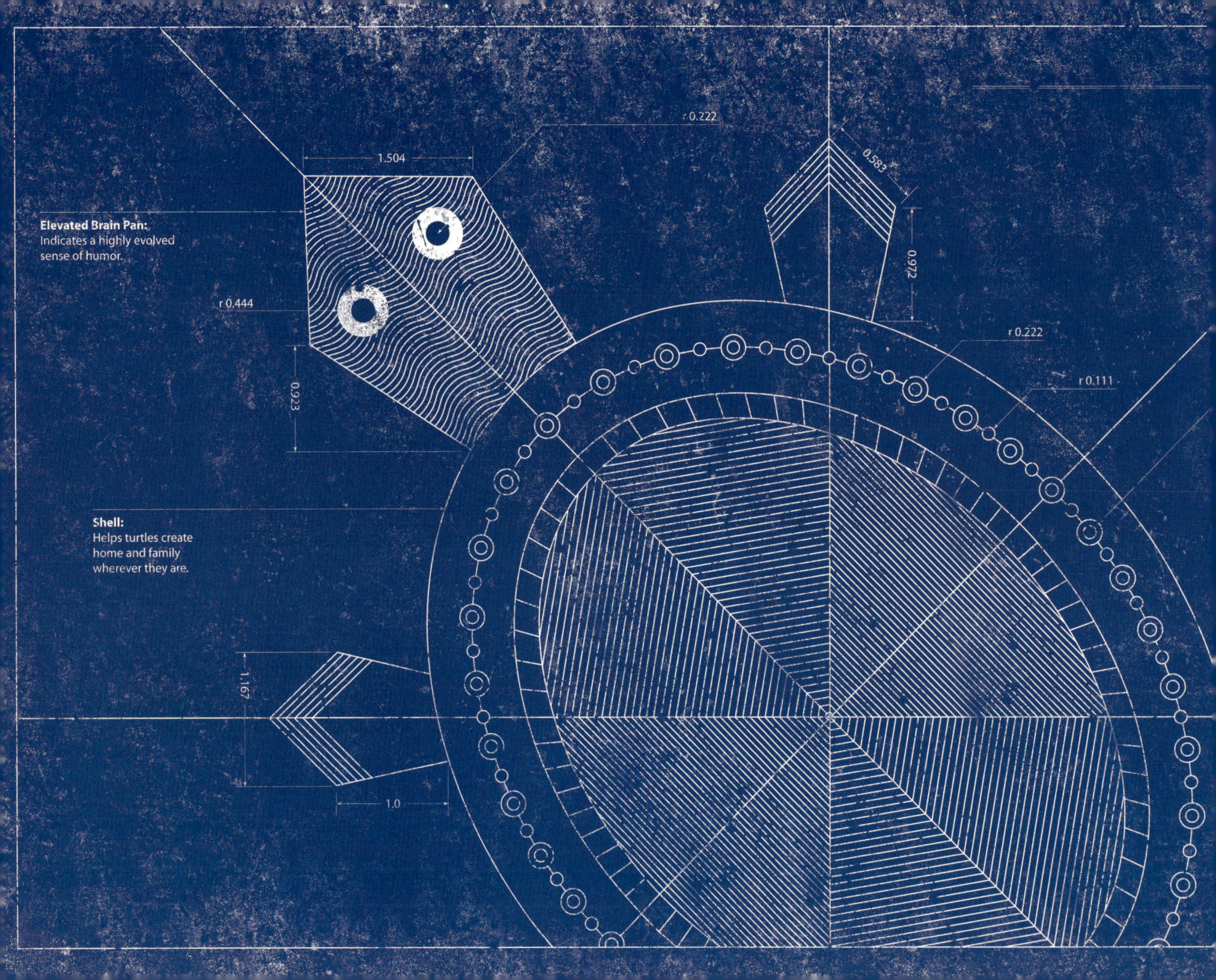

Elevated Brain Pan:
Indicates a highly evolved sense of humor.

Shell:
Helps turtles create home and family wherever they are.

AUDIO TRACK NUMBER FOUR

KNOWING
WHO THEY ARE

If you believe that the brightest star is only seen through the shadow of night,
If you believe that the color of truth is neither black nor white,
If you believe that to walk in darkness is the first step toward the light,
Then believe that confusion and chaos are the gifts that will shape your life.
If you believe like the smallest of seeds that gets tossed in the breeze
   to finally blossom on earth,
So shall the lost and lonely soul find the miracle of rebirth.
You may travel an easy road but ev'ry now and then you must fly
   thru' the eye of the storm,
To finally reach the rainbow's end,
If you believe.
If you believe that to find true happiness you must first have had a broken heart,
If you believe that to finally reach your dreams, sometimes your life
   must fall apart,
If you believe that all things are possible, no matter who or where you are,
Then you have found the spirit within you
to give birth to a dancing star, to a dancing star!

To A Dancing Star
music: Robert Seeley
lyrics: Robert Espindola

Scale 1:1/16

Detailed Patterning: indicates an over-developed sense of style.

Tough Skin: Evolved as a defense against the "slings and arrows" of life.

0.964

Soft Underbelly & Compassionate Heart: (See tough skin.)

illustration: Joseph Rattan/Glenn Hadsall

KNOWING WHO THEY ARE

In a letter to Graham Munson, author Radclyffe Hall (*The Well of Loneliness*, 1928) wrote: "I realize that (notoriety) is the price I must pay for having intentionally come out into the open…" She goes on to describe the price each person pays: "Nothing is so spiritually degrading or so undermining of one's morale as living a lie, as keeping friends only by false pretences." Before trying to publish, Hall consulted her partner, Una Troubridge, certain that indignant bluestockings wouldn't stop at attacking only the author of such a book, acting on suppositions about her lifestyle that were all too true. Troubridge's answer was courageous and eloquent: "I told her to write what was in her heart, that so far as any effect upon myself was concerned, I was sick to death of ambiguities, and only wished to be known for what I was and to dwell with her in the palace of truth."

Many political battles have been fought and some have been won, yet fear and distrust of gay people still thrives, primarily because of the religious right and crusades against "degenerates" by people like Jerry Falwell. So coming out is still difficult and painful for some men, and a lot depends on when and with whom—as a young man, during a career, while married? Completely or in stages?

T. Michael Chandler has a gay brother and many gay relatives in his family. His mother always knew he was gay, and Chandler knew it from childhood. His family has always supported his life choices and allowed him to develop his own criteria for emotional wellbeing. Similarly, Jim Ross came from a very sophisticated background, growing up in the Denver area with a mother who was a Unitarian. Jim came out to her inadvertently when he told her where he was working and she recognized it as a gay bar that she had visited with one of her gay friends. Jim's sister is an ardent feminist who thinks it's cool that Jim is gay and his employers and friends have been supportive, though he came out to them in stages. When Kenn McBryde came out to his family years ago, he displayed the same quiet courage he still displays as someone who has been HIV-positive for fifteen years (and feels well and looks terrific). "My mom and I went through all the stages of grief in two or three hours. I said, 'Mom, you and daddy have taught me to be myself, and myself is a gay man, that's who I am. If you want me to be myself that's who I have to be.' And they pretty much have been supportive since then."

For all the men, joining the TCC represents an avowal of their orientation. Jason Walker had to struggle with his decision to join for five years. (The poem "I Can Breathe Again" tells the story.) A concert by the Chorale is a good way to broach the subject of orientation with parents or relatives when it's hard to get the

Only five days after our nation suffered the staggering losses of 9/11, the Chorale joined with The Women's Chorus of Dallas to perform A Musical Healing Concert that raised in excess of $16,000 for the Red Cross. The Grace United Methodist Church was packed with people flowing out onto the lawn. It was truly a time of healing for singers and listeners.

The chorale has always kept music as its main focus. But the mission of the chorale, to make a difference in the world through its singing, sometimes takes public form as pictured here. The chorale helped organize and perform for the *Defend, Don't Amend* rally to protect the constitution. Pictured are singers and partners Tim Blanchard-Modisette and Pat Blanchard-Modisette.

They are being filmed for a documentary on the TCC to be aired on PBS.

You captured our hearts, and in one stroke of the artist's brush, illuminated our minds....

I will always remember the first number that your choir literally burst upon the stage with: "Open Wide." It reminded me so of that evening ten years ago when my 18-year-old son burst into the house and declared to his entire family that he was gay. I did not quite understand his enthusiasm, until now. The song allowed me to feel, perhaps for the very first time, the burden he must have felt keeping such an intrinsic part of his being a secret--and his joy when that burden was lifted!

Joseph's Grandmother and Great Aunts were in attendance at the concert. The look of astonishment on their faces at the beautiful sounds you created was a joy to see. To hear them speak of your group so lovingly, filled with pride that their nephew was a member, and to watch as over 375 collective years of ignorance faded from view filled my heart with love.

You captured our hearts, and in one stroke of the artist's brush, illuminated our minds to the struggles and tribulations all of you must have had to overcome. I salute your performance.

I have never been more proud of my son, and although we lost Joseph's father during the Vietnam Conflict, I know that he, too, is beaming at the man his son has become. A man unafraid to face an ignorant society, boldly--armed only with his belief in God, a beautiful voice, and the most tender of souls.

Ester J. Hailey
October 25, 1989

Incredible small groups and precision ensembles are a signature of the TCC. Pictured are the Stars and Stripes Forever Lawn Chair Brigade and (below) the Turtle Creek Strangerettes rehearsing sans costumes.

24

words out. Dozens of letters and stories from members tell of estrangements ended when loved ones were invited to a concert. Parents' imaginations sometimes run riot when their children are telling them that they're different, and the telling becomes a confession even when there's nothing to confess. It's much easier to say, "I'm like these men, these are my brothers" when they are clearly an elect company of talented, committed idealists. Ultimately, even parents who have tried very hard not to understand will have to respect their son for his achievements, share in his successes and appreciate his music.

Coming out to wives and children can be a shattering experience. Yet many Chorale members are fast friends with their ex-wives and close to their children. New member John Connell describes his wife's reaction when he came out to her. "That explains a lot. But you know, my dear, I know that you are who you are. And this is who you are." He still adores her and they are the best of friends. John came out to his youngest daughter in September of '02 and her sister in February of '03, telling each the same thing: "the only regret in my life is that your mother was not loved as fully as she deserved." Hearing this, both daughters' response was the same: "But daddy, neither were you."

The Chorale may be more or less important as a refuge according to what individual members are going through in their personal lives, but from the beginning all see it as an opportunity for creative expression and a means to accomplish important goals—goals which are soon identified with the mission of the Chorale, accomplished as the Chorale evolves, making new friends, building new bridges.

Bert Martin cites two experiences that transformed how he felt about the mission of the Chorale. Twelve years or so ago at the GALA convention in Denver, ACT UP was going to protest gay choruses who didn't identify themselves as such. The protesters planned to turn their backs on the Turtle Creek Chorale, blow whistles and get themselves ejected. However, the message of the Chorale in the song they sang about AIDS was so powerful that the protest never came off. The TCC established itself as one of the first to sing about the loss of loved ones to AIDS and it has continued to take on social issues in its songs and carry its message to the people who most need to hear it.

Bert cites the concert in Prague as a life-changing experience for him—as it was for the Czechs who came to the concert. Under communism, women found to be gay went to prison, and men went to prison with hard labor. "Our concert was the first to benefit AIDS, this was the first time people had bought a ticket to benefit gay people. It would be like buying a ticket to benefit polygamy in this country. Well, at the end of the concert, the Lucille Ball of their country came onstage and held hands with us, and we sang 'We Shall Overcome' with the Czechs following along as best they could. It was incredible…the older people especially looked scared, but then their jubilation kept breaking through. You saw it happening right there on their faces. They looked stunned but they couldn't hide how happy they felt."

While the men rehearse and refine, and while their audiences don't vary much in size, people are always discovering them, hearing them on a CD and talking about them everywhere. Could they step away from their lives and get a sense of what is happening, surely they would feel how important they've become to more and more people, not just at home, where people can't wait for the next concert and count on the Chorale to keep them coming, but all over the world where people who've heard a little just want more.

Thus the Chorale is giving its members the chance to make more of a difference by continuing to be themselves, and that's why there's an undercurrent of quiet excitement in what the men say about their lives, a sense that they are going in the right direction, have perhaps seen glimmers of an open society that would thrive on mutual respect. One senses that more freedom will be possible for them just by keeping on, and more joy, so that their decision to live in the "palace of truth" will continue to be vindicated as more and more people are moved by their voices, touched by what they have to say and delighted to know them as they are.

Dressing up is always something the Chorale enjoys, whether it is in tux or as depicted here at a recent concert of the music of Elton John. Each member dressed as his favorite incarnation of Elton.

For more than 15 years, the TCC has memorialized the members it has lost by presenting one poinsettia plant for each at the holiday concert. Over 140 singers have been lost so far, mostly to complications from AIDS. Shown with the chorus is singing member Keith Arcement. Keith is also shown in a former life as a Benedictine monk. The singers come from every walk of life imaginable.

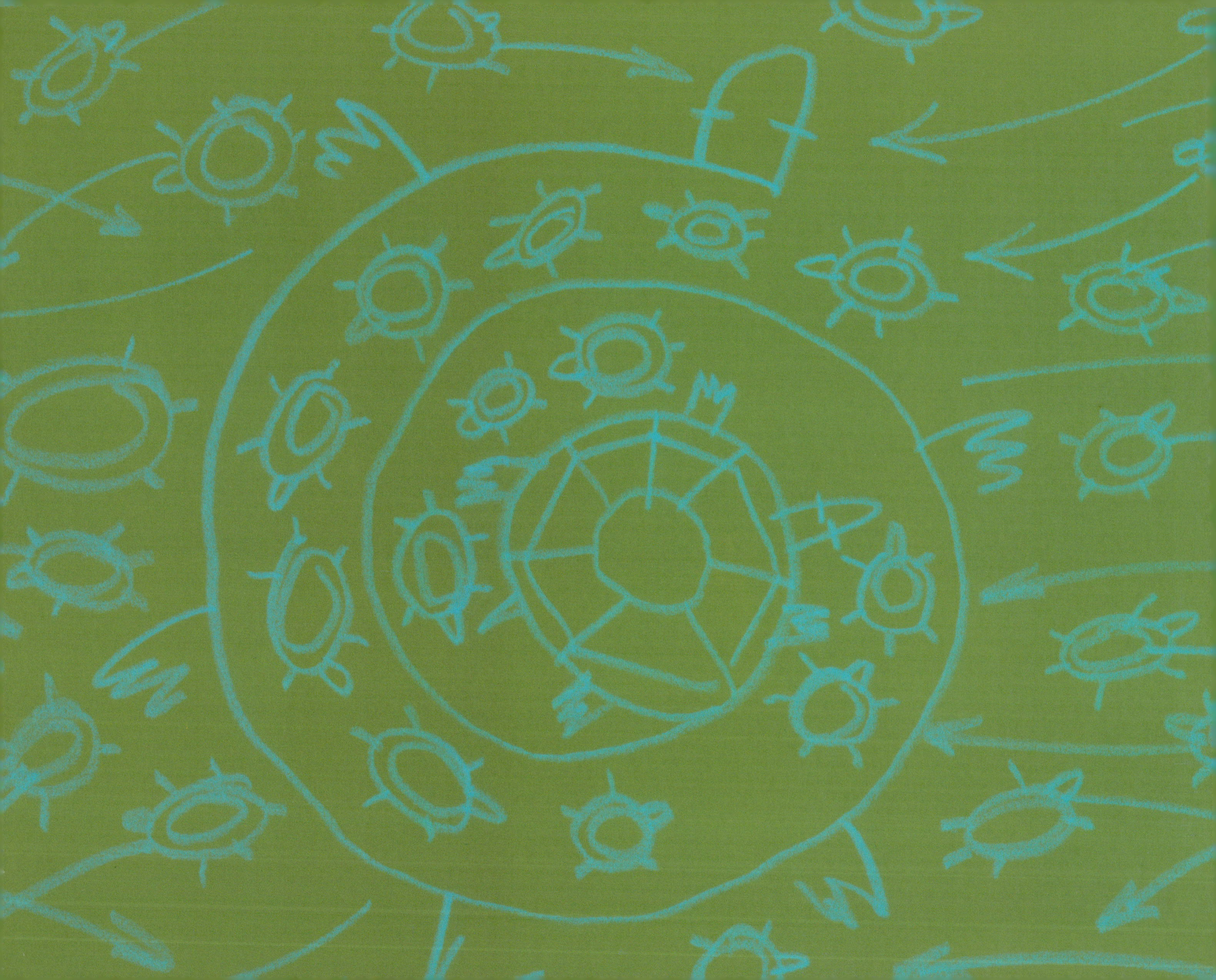

AUDIO TRACK NUMBER FIVE

Caring
FOR THEIR COMMUNITY

I shall miss loving you.
I shall miss loving you.
I shall miss the comfort of your embrace.
The comfort of your embrace.
I shall miss loving you.
I shall miss loving you
I shall miss the loneliness of waiting for the calls
That never came.
I shall miss the joy of your comings
I shall miss the pain of your goings, and, after a time.
I shall miss missing loving you.
I shall miss loving you.
I shall miss the comfort of your embrace.
The comfort of your embrace.
I shall miss the comfort, and, after a time
I shall miss missing loving you.

I Shall Miss Loving You
from *After Goodbye: An AIDS Story*
music: Kris Anthony
lyrics: Peter McWilliams

illustration: Joseph Rattan

CARING FOR THEIR COMMUNITY

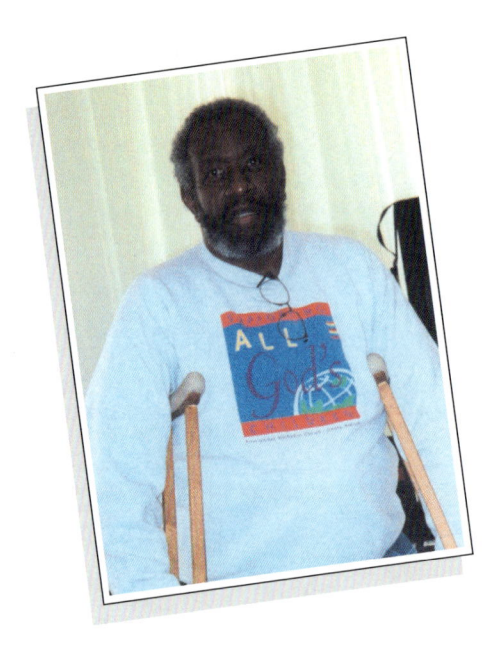

Through the years, the members of the TCC have suffered losses far beyond what most groups experience. Beyond the ravages of HIV, other issues beset the members. Fred Moore has been a singing member of the TCC for 20 years. His health problems have taken both of his legs, and yet he has only missed a handful of concerts in all that time. When he does miss one, the audience members certainly notice, as does Tim. Fred IS the low bass section.

Caring is a way of life for the Turtle Creek Chorale—and its reason for being. It may not be a reason for joining but the new member soon knows that he has been adopted by a caring family. His new brothers care about everything that has happened to him and everything that is about to happen. His big buddy will tell him what he needs to know about the rules. He'll receive his music packet and sing a little. But he will quickly realize that his voice—whether beautiful or untrained and ordinary—isn't the reason his colleagues care. From day one he's a person, not just a voice. He is the very person the Chorale is singing about in "To a Dancing Star": So whatever you need to share, whatever you need to say, know that there is someone who will never turn away.

And now he's singing it. Yet there's a lot to learn about caring. He may already have heard about John Thomas, former head of the AIDS Resources Center and a founding member of the TCC, who died of AIDS in 1999 at age 51. Though his illness forced him to withdraw from the center in 1995, he continued fundraising and gaining support for a variety of causes until the last year of his life. Many who loved him may have been troubled by his decision to refuse AIDS drugs, then life-support that would have made the end easier. Some may have understood that he needed to die as he had lived, facing all challenges with his naked humanity and goodness, embracing friend and foe with the same warmth. His friendliness and openness were more than a tactic that made divisive posturing impossible. The people he touched were able to glimpse a better world: he showed how love could create patience, and how an approach tempered by patience could lead to understanding—sooner than the most brilliant pressure strategies and logical (or hysterical) demonstrations of just cause. Obviously he believed that we were put here to love and be loved, not merely to be right.

What was said of Mr. Thomas after his death is revelatory, especially since the words came from men who became activists—or became better activists—because of his example. "Some spark each of us recognized in him can be recognized in ourselves..." (Gary Lanham, his partner); "God bless big lovable fools like John who think they can change the world. Because they can..." (William Waybourn). At his memorial service, Tim Seelig read from e-mails and letters Thomas received after he stopped treatment. Among them the following stands out: "Love leaves behind more than death takes away."

At the chorale retreat in 2003, each member who had passed away was memorialized with his name on a star, hanging above the heads of the singers the entire weekend. Later, at a holiday performance, the TCC singers repeated this tribute by wearing stars with the names on them.

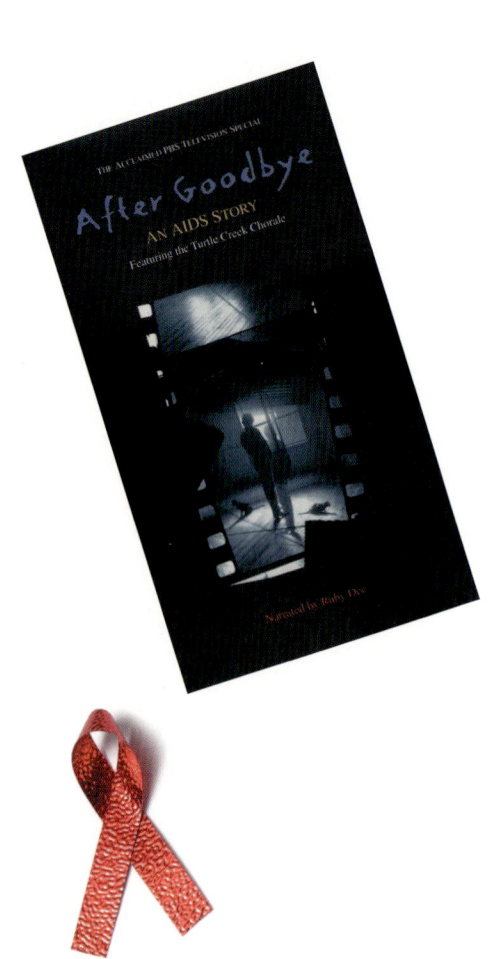

The symbols of our losses were everywhere. The TCC began to wear AIDS awareness pins as a part of the standard tuxedo. It also made its first quilt panel in 1988 with 12 names on it.

33

THE TORTOISE SOCIETY was created to recognize those who have chosen to leave a future legacy to the TCC. Membership in the society honors those who have included the Turtle Creek Chorale as a part of their estate planning. By remembering the Turtle Creek Chorale in a will, through an insurance policy or retirement plan, by establishing a charitable remainder trust or through any other planned-giving vehicle, TCC friends have the opportunity to ensure their appreciation, support, and love of the organization lives on in perpetuity.

- Jo & Ralph Blackburn
  - T. Michael Chandler
    - Randal Eaton Culbreth
- Robert Forner & Erin Thorkildsen
  - Dan Dixon & Bob Ivancic
    - Chet Flake & Bud Knight
- David Fleming
  - The Estate of Sam Frech
    - Victor Ray & Randal G. Ray
- John M. Henrikson
  - C. Dooley Hitch
    - Robert Alan Huneke
- Bruce W. Jaster
  - W. A. & Glenda K. Jaster Estate
    - Jeff Johnston
- Jack E. Kaiser
  - Paul Kolasci III
    - Gordon M. Markley
- Joseph Gale Pacetti
  - Michael L. Rogers
    - Mrs. Mary Dell Talley
- Kay Wilkinson
  - The Estate of Kirby Wyatt

REQUIEM
TURTLE CREEK CHORALE

Always a friend, during the latter days of his illness Thomas had a profound influence on Dr. Seelig. With his many talents, Tim had always succeeded by lighting a fire under people—inspiring them by his example—but Thomas helped to confirm the wisdom of the approach that has worked best with the Chorale: helping members to find the spark in themselves. That spark is present today in many Chorale members' lives, still putting out the kind of energy that will "change the world one heart (or consciousness) at a time."

Shortly after joining, one member was moved to write the following to Tim Seelig: "I'm just floored by how much you CARE about us. Not just us as a whole and how we sound, but on the one-to-one level as well…It's a new experience to me, and I'm feeling quite blessed to have that in my life."

Even though he may not have any special needs of his own at the time, the new member will become aware of the Special Needs Committee which tries to assure that sickness or injury or economic hardship doesn't isolate members of the family. Thus members can be assured of a ride to rehearsal when their car breaks down, someone to cut the grass when they're in the hospital or cook a meal when they're bedridden at home. Another member had this to say about the support he received from "the guys" after a serious accident: "You don't even know what some of them have been willing to do. I've had guys call me almost daily to check on me…They've given me rides to rehearsal and back home. They've let me stay in their homes for the weekend so that I could have a chance to get out of the house for a while…My own father has not called me once since I've been out of the hospital, but you all have been there. It's been incredible!"

In the Chorale caring is active, one doesn't "feel the pain" of another without doing something about it. Small kindnesses resonate. A member who suffers from fibromyalgia described a wardrobe problem that nearly kept him out of a concert. He decided he'd show up no matter what, and spent a lot of time rigging his clothes to make a smooth change. Yet when the time came he was having trouble getting into his tux. Then "a member of our family I don't even know saw I was having trouble dealing with studs and my bow tie and…helped me out of my ordeal…He left my pride intact! I know that seems insignificant…but it was and is a big deal to me. We ARE family!"

Caring for the entire community through song is a daunting and exhausting task. The chorus also spends a great amount of time with internal caregiving. Shown enjoying a little R&R are TCC members on a beach outside Barcelona during the European tour and posing in front of a fountain in Montreal.

A letter from real estate broker Paul LaPierre indicates why the Chorale's style of caring has made it a breeding ground for activists. After the breakup of an eight-year relationship which had been the reason for relocating to Dallas, he writes "I had never felt so alone. In calling my family for support, my sister's reaction was 'I don't understand why you're so upset.' We had no societal affirmation of our relationship, therefore in her blind eyes, there was no relationship. …In contrast, my father compared my pain to the pain he felt when my mother died. So…I will rally to protect our constitution from being amended to exclude a segment of our society from certain rights." A real estate broker *demonstrating*? But then, John Thomas was a lifelong Republican.

To concert-goers, mindful of the charitable purposes of the Chorale, caring has a different look and feel. That the men are volunteers indicates caring, that they have worked so hard to perform impeccably indicates caring. The sign interpretation by Don Jones is caring personified. And in a concert to raise funds for people with AIDS the realization may come that part of the Chorale's fresh sound has been created by men living with AIDS. As practiced by the Chorale, caring stays ahead of pity, even self-pity, and tries never to look back. "We are all in this together," they seem to be saying. "Yes, many of us are bereft or bereaved, too many have been cut down, but we refuse to see any cruelty in this. We are focused on what we love in life and we are finding it in each other. This love doesn't stop with us. It is shared with those who come to hear us. They can feel it."

Michael Messmer has lived close to twenty years with AIDS. Along with his cane he carries quite a bit of medicine around, yet there's a happy sparkle in his eyes. It wasn't always so. Around the time of "Sing for the Cure" (June, 2000), he was despondent. He still had his family to live for but felt his life slipping away. Then he heard Maya Angelou reading Pam Martin's narrative about a choice all of us have to make, all who are faced with a life-threatening disease. Either we will mope about the abyss ahead or we'll laugh about it, laugh about the whole situation, dance right up to the edge of annihilation, laughing. "I started to cry," says Michael. "We're not supposed to cross that line but I couldn't help it. Still, I knew that I wanted to laugh. I made that choice. I wasn't going to sit around and cry. You don't turn over that leaf easily. I didn't laugh any that day. But it did make me want to go farther." Thanks to the Chorale Michael feels that he has been able to "Help people, not just me. It took away the anguish and bitterness and gave me a little more healing power." And where does he go from here? "I want to be a force for healing. That's what I live for… I do a little hospice work on the side."

*My life is about how I can make a difference
in the world, or even one person's life today....*

What we did today at University Baptist Church in Austin, was not a performance in my book, but a pure and unconditional outpouring of love. Is there anything stronger than that? I recently put myself on triple combination therapy. It has turned out to be much more of an ordeal than I thought it would be. I was in severe discomfort at both of our Tony performances. In the last month I have lost many hours of sleep. My wonderfully supportive mother has told me over and over in the last month to "keep my chin up," and it has been really hard. I cried cleansing and healing tears all the way home from Austin as I reflected on the wonderful thing that happened there. I am so grateful to be a part of an organization that lifts my chin up when I just don't feel like holding it up myself.

Finally, I want you to know this about me: my life is not about how pretty my boyfriend is, how many digits my salary is, or what people think of me. My life is about how I can make a difference in the world or even one person's life today. I just wanted to take a moment to thank you for allowing me the opportunity to make a difference.

with all my love and gratitude
Rob Jerger
June 7, 1998

During the Fall of 2003, the chorale was privileged to perform at the 2 X 2 Art for AIDS Auction where guests of honor were Liza Minelli and Dr. Mathilde Krim, founder of the American Foundation for AIDS Research. (Tim forgot the chorus was singing when the cameras starting flashing....good thing the chorus doesn't really need him all that much!)
(opposite) The Chorale performs at one of the regional displays of the Quilt Project AIDS Memorial.

39

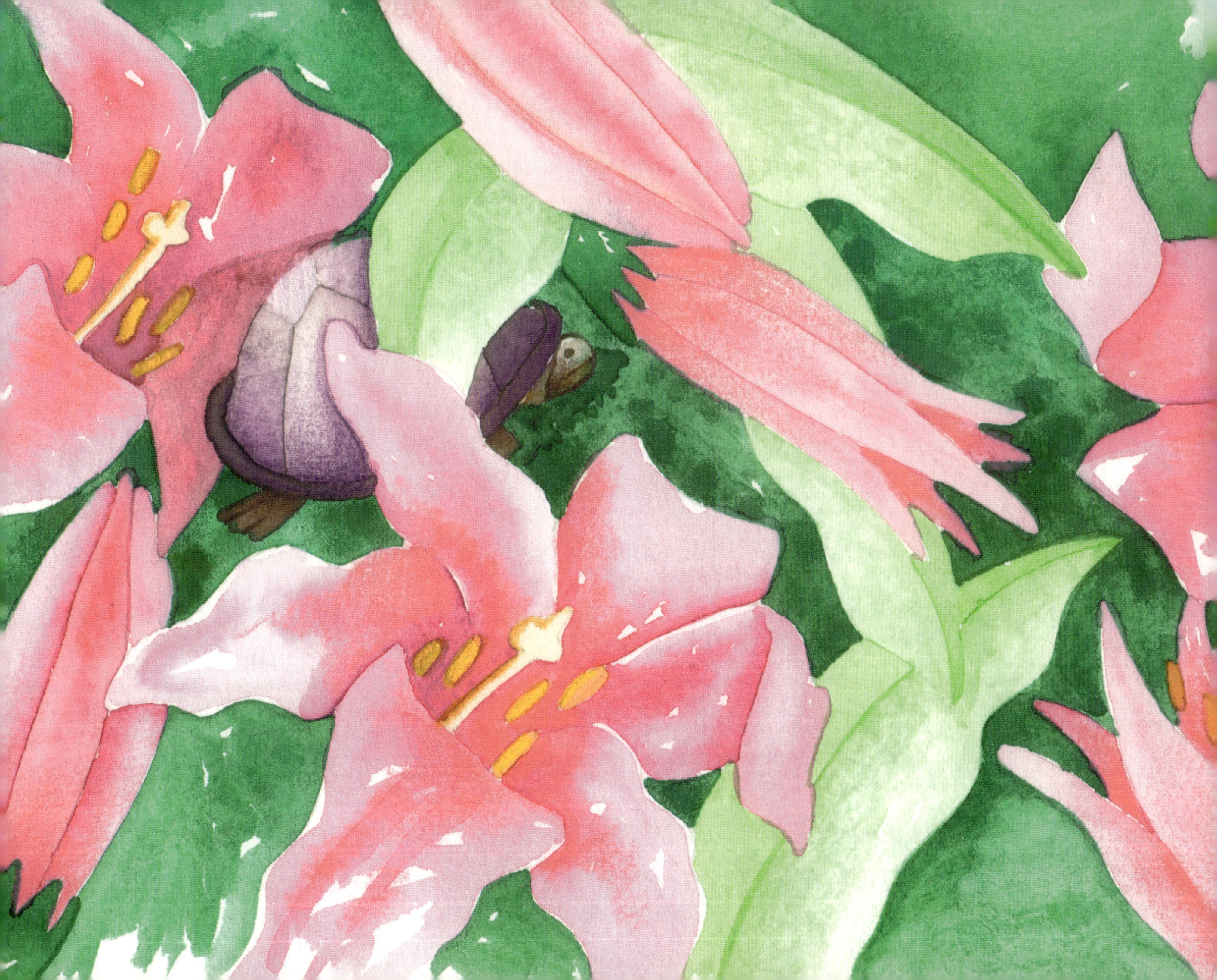

AUDIO TRACK NUMBER SIX

Reaching

OUT TO THE WOMEN IN THEIR LIVES

Come to me, mother, again in my dreams.
Lie down beside me once more while you sing.
Soothe all my troubles and come ease my pain.
Speak to me, mother, and whisper my name.
Was I to blame, mother?
Why did you go leaving me lonely and missing you so?
You left an emptiness no one can feel.
Don't you know, mother, that I love you still?
Come to me, mother, again while I sleep.
Comfort and hold me once more while I weep.
Nothing can lessen the longing, it seems.
Come to me, mother, again in my dreams.

Come To Me, Mother
music: Jill Gallina
lyrics: Pamela Martin

illustration: Joseph Rattan

REACHING OUT TO THE WOMEN IN THEIR LIVES

In 1980, when the Turtle Creek Chorale was founded, the only thought was to have a men's chorus. In fact, the men's and women's communities did not commingle much in those days. Each was finding its own way and spent its free time outside work fairly segregated. In general, all activities were done quietly in Dallas, and mostly indoors. It would be several years until there was even a "Freedom Parade" (what most cities called Gay Pride).

All that changed in 1989 when Dr. Timothy Seelig, in his second year as artistic director of the TCC, met with a friend of his and together founded The Women's Chorus of Dallas. Ralph Blackburn remembers that it was after the Seattle GALA convention that Tim got together with some of the women. The feeling was, if the men had the Chorale, why couldn't the women have something like it? The early going wasn't easy. Sibling rivalry? Of course. This nine-year-old boy suddenly had a new baby in the house getting all the attention.

With the passing years, the women began to work alongside the men in the struggle against AIDS, as many of their friends were affected. At the GALA convention in Tampa eight years ago, the women's chorus joined the Chorale onstage—dramatizing how much the brother had accepted the younger sister, and how their respective communities in Dallas had changed. These two choruses have also changed Dallas in that the men's and women's communities now work much more closely together. By 2004, The Women's Chorus of Dallas has made seven recordings in collaboration with the Turtle Creek Chorale.

In 1998, the women's chorus lost its first member, Jeri Lynne Smith, to breast cancer, and the two choruses pulled closer together out of shared pain. In 1999, a Chorale member's mother was fighting breast cancer as well. He suggested a change in the red ribbons that the Chorale had been wearing to signify AIDS awareness. A red and pink ribbon would signify the Chorale's willingness to reciprocate the support the women had shown them in the fight against AIDS. At the debut of Old Turtle, the new ribbons became official. Gary Rifkin describes what happened: "It was a very moving ceremony. The women were onstage with us when the switch was announced, and the women who were standing next to the guys officially 'pinned' us. I will never forget the tears I could not hold back as one of my 'sisters' stood there and put the new red and pink ribbon pin on my lapel."

The singers were thrilled to make their 2nd appearance at Carnegie Hall in 2002. The Chorale was honored to present *Sing for the Cure* for the Komen Foundation's 20th Anniversary celebration.

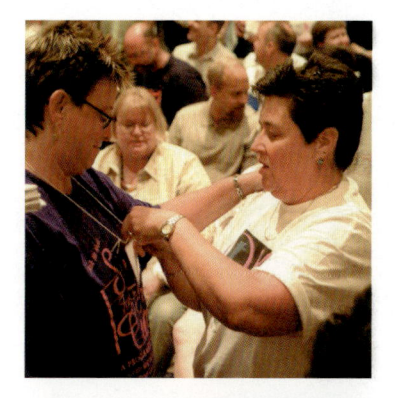

To better reach out to the women in our community, the Chorale voted unanimously to change the red AIDS-awareness ribbon the singers had worn for many years to red and pink to denote the Chorale's awareness of its sisters and their fight against breast cancer. When the change was made, they actually pinned each other in a moving ceremony.

As *Sing for the Cure* swept the nation, it was performed hundreds of times in many arenas. One performance provided an exciting opportunity for Dr. Seelig to sing the final number, *One Voice,* to kick off the national *Race for the Cure* on the mall in Washington, D.C. There was an estimated crowd of 100,000. While TCC and TWCD were performing SFTC at Carnegie Hall, the group showed up in the chilly wee hours of the morning in order to be at the front of the group gathered for the NBC Morning Show. It made quite an impression on the host anchors and got great coverage for *Sing for the Cure* as well. Janey Hall tried to block Tim from view, but they settled their turf battles just as the camera clicked.

We will keep on singing
'til the ribbons that we wear
Wave like banners of life,
Wave like banners in the air.

AUDIO TRACK NUMBER SEVEN

When "Sing for the Cure" was commissioned by the Susan G. Komen Foundation, ten composers were chosen to write ten compositions for a symphonic cycle to lyrics by Pamela Martin of Austin (such as the excerpt above). Dr. Maya Angelou read the narration that Pam also wrote chronicling the issues and effects of the progressive disease in the minds of the community, of partners, and through the voices of the sister, the mother, the children affected. Along the way many questions are posed that can't be answered…Who will speak?…Is this the borrowed time?…Where are (the shining stars) now? Was I to blame, mother?…Don't you know that I love you still?…Who will curl my daughter's hair, hear her prayers, sing her lullabies? And the questions are answered the way the Chorale answers the questions it raises: We will keep on singing 'til we're heard, 'til our work is done, 'til our race is won… "We will keep on singing 'til the ribbons that we wear wave like banners of life, wave like banners in the air."

From its beginning with the Turtle Creek Chorale, "Sing for the Cure" has swept the country. Gay and lesbian choruses are featured in about 10 percent of these performances. The Chorale helped to pass the torch to other choruses with its performance at the GALA convention in San Jose—in a limited space—so that other choruses wouldn't be deterred from performing the work because of limited budgets or choral resources. Four years after the first "Sing for the Cure" the spirit and intention that gave life to the music is still reaching out to Americans, particularly women, who most need to hear its message.

In 2003, a mixed chorus was born—One Achord—which brings men and women together for the first time as part of the Turtle Creek Chorale. So while the healing from "Sing for the Cure" still ripples across the land—along with other cooperative ventures such as Old Turtle and John Rutter's Requiem (that hit Billboard's Top 10 classical recordings chart)—these men and women are exploring new ways to make waves. Drawing on a tradition of attending each other's concerts, recording together and singing together for the Human Rights Campaign, discussions are now underway to put both choruses under the same umbrella so that their resources will not be needlessly duplicated.

In the year that marked the founding of The Women's Chorus of Dallas, Anne Albritton, its principal accompanist and arranger, began her long association with Dr. Seelig as Artistic Director (twelve years with the women's chorus and another six years as principal accompanist of the Turtle Creek Chorale, where she's a Life Member). Because of illness, she retired from the TCC four years ago, after the performances in San Jose.

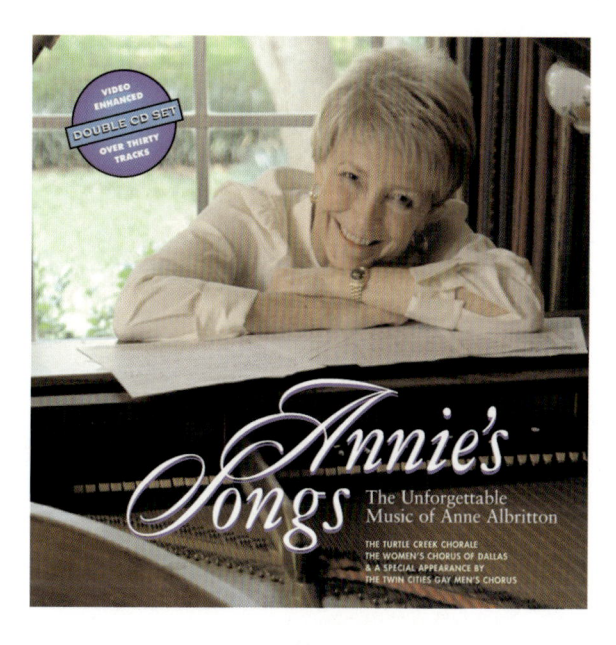

Longtime accompanist, composer and arranger Anne Albritton also became mom, sister and 'girlfriend' to hundreds of singers through her years with the TCC. Upon her diagnosis with cancer, the chorus released a double CD of her arrangements to honor her and assist with medical costs.

When a performance can speak to people's souls as well as their hearts and minds, you have been a complete success....

In January, my mother died of cancer. She was a strong and wonderful person who demanded that her life be positive, forward-looking, constructive and humor-filled. She also demanded that tears and emotion not be wasted in looking back and being sad when she died. At her funeral, I desperately needed to cry, but didn't feel that I had her permission to do so.

When I heard "Sing For The Cure," there was a message that met all of my mother's requirements—it was forward-looking (working for a cure), humor-filled (respectful but not maudlin). I tried to be quiet as the emotions flooded over me throughout the evening. Tears flowed.

I was finally able to cry for my mama! They were not sad, mournful tears, but represented the happy, hopeful, uplifting recognition of a life well-lived. All that was good, warm, funny and marvelous about my mama returned. I've moved on and dealt with a large void in the center of my soul. When a performance can speak to people's souls as well as their hearts and minds, you have been a complete success.

I am a peaceful, happier and better person for spending Saturday evening in Dallas with the Turtle Creek Chorale.

from a letter to Tim Seelig
from a "Sing For The Cure"
concert attendee

Members, especially the basses that sat behind her night after night and understood the meaning of every hand signal, often mention the warmth that radiated from "little Annie" in their letters. The men never had to reach very far for help from her—she was right there with them from note to note and many of them thought of her as "mom." In recognition of all she has contributed, the Chorale's next CD (its 33rd) will consist entirely of songs she has composed or arranged for TCC and TWCD. Gratefully, groups within the Choruses have underwritten individual songs on the new CD. Educators within the TCC have sponsored "I have loved." Health care workers of the TCC/TWCD are sponsoring "When October Goes."

Finally, the Chorale recognizes a debt to some of the women who have become stalwart supporters of the Chorale, attending, donating, making their homes or their time available to members who have reached out to them. For Kenn McBryde, the McDermott sisters, Susie and Honey, are simply his best friends. Susie was someone Kenn knew from work years ago, he met her sister later. The three of them are inseparable; the women wouldn't go shopping without him. Since Kenn began to work for the Chorale some years ago as their "computer guy" he decided he wanted to separate his work from his singing; when he's with the Chorale he wants to sing, when he's at the office he wants to work, and when he's got some free time, he wants to spend it with the McDermotts. Their friendship began with a love of music, and a love of the Chorale, and that has sustained it, along with their obvious affection for each other. Kenn and his friends are mentioned here to show that, although the Chorale is a family, it's not a private club, and the large size of this family has never in the least constrained its willingness to adopt.

Reaching out to the women in our lives happened both on and off stage. The Women's Chorus of Dallas became partners, not only in our performances and recordings, but in our hearts.

These photos show the founder of the Komen Foundation, Nancy Brinker, thanking the TCC and TWCD for the gift of their music. A tribute to the people honored by *Sing for the Cure* is shown at the far right.

TURTLE CREEK CHORALE

SING FOR THE CURE

WITH THE WOMEN'S CHORUS OF DALLAS
CELEBRATING THE TWENTIETH ANNIVERSARY OF THE
SUSAN G. KOMEN BREAST CANCER FOUNDATION.

The Women's Chorus of Dallas has made a name for itself in the 16 years it has been making music. Their beautiful tone is legendary and their performances are exciting and heart-warming as well. At work or at play, these women are important in the life of the Turtle Creek Chorale.

50

The two groups, TCC and TWCD, not only perform live, but have recorded together, producing an important opus of works for mixed chorus. Pictured at left, clockwise from center are: *Family, Sing For The Cure, Song Of Wisdom From Old Turtle, Comfort & Joy, Annie's Songs - The Unforgettable Music Of Anne Albritton, Lifelong Friend, Let Music Live,* and *Requiem* by John Rutter.

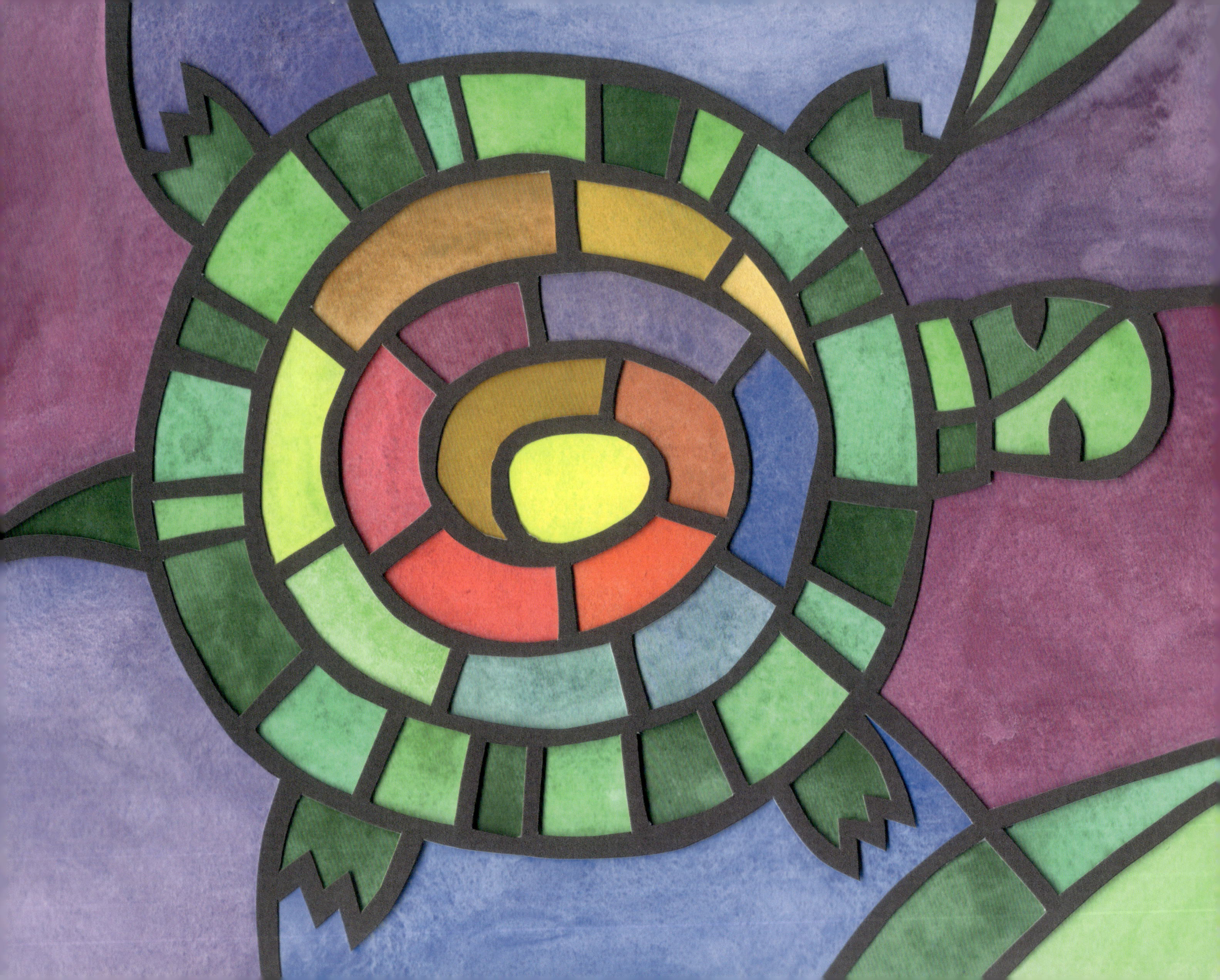

AUDIO TRACK NUMBER EIGHT

Building
BRIDGES OF UNDERSTANDING

When you dwell in the secret place in the secret place of the Most High,
You live safely under the shadow of the Almighty
I will say to my Creator "You are my hiding place
You are my hiding place; My God in whom I trust"
Surely he will release me from traps that would enslave me;
Surely he will defend me from violence in the streets;
He will save me, he will redeem me, he will rescue me, he will deliver me
My Creator will cover me with her feathers and under her wings I will be safe
She will guide, she will guide me past the hands that reach out death to me,
That reach out death to me
She will protect me from the plague that threatens all I love;
She will hold me in her arms, she will hold me through the night,
She will hold me through the lonely, restless night, through the night,
In her arms
God's truth will guard me from the lies of my enemy,
I will take my stand against them unafraid,
Because I have found a safe place, a sanctuary, a refuge in my Creator,
In my Creator, the most high God
My Creator knows my name, and calls out to me, "I love you. I love you.
I love you. I love you."

A Secret Place / Psalm 91
music: Danny Ray
lyrics: adaped by Dr. Mel White

illustration: Joseph Rattan

BUILDING BRIDGES OF UNDERSTANDING

Tiffany Roberts stunned holiday audiences with her impeccable coloratura soprano and infectious smile. The TCC has been honored to encourage many young singers throughout its history. In fact, two such discoveries, LaTonia Moore and Jesus Garcia, now sing regularly at the Metropolitan Opera.

Chorale members love to sing, this is one thing they all have in common. In addition, they want their songs to be taken seriously, and not just because they sing them well. Over time they've learned that some people will change the way they feel about them through the messages and emotions in their music, and that's where bridges come in. Bridges have come to symbolize a way of reaching other groups directly, particularly traditional religious institutions, charities, and occupational or cultural groups that play a role in all of our lives. The point is access, nothing more: the chance to be heard, the chance to be themselves. Their expectations are modest. They don't expect to be loved or lionized, but they've also learned over time that some people will understand their songs, and because of these people, the love in their songs and the meaning in them will be magnified. Before long, people will be crossing the bridge the other way, inspired in their turn to give the gift of themselves.

A bridge is a technical marvel. Many bridges never get past the planning stage; others are abandoned because of problems at the other end, real or imaginary. Bridges seem like the right idea to people on both sides but fears arise, especially when the Chorale seems to be "converting" someone from the other side, as may have been the case when gospel singer Cynthia Clawson was forced to pull out of a concert with the Chorale because of threats from fundamentalist Christians, or when Dallas's huge First Baptist Church—on moral grounds—refused to allow the Chorale to perform at the invitation of a choral convention being held at the church. The huge First Methodist Church a few blocks away opened its doors to the standing room only crowd.

One of the architects of a sturdy bridge that went up in July 2001 was Gary Rifkin of the Chorale. A member of the National Speakers Association, he conceived of the bridge when his group announced its national convention would be held in Dallas. When he went to pick up National Vice President Chris Clarke-Epstein at the airport (18 months before the convention) she was blown away by the "Sounds of the Sixties" CD Gary conveniently had playing in his car. She thought the convention chair should hear what the Chorale was doing, and told him. It was decided: The Turtle Creek Chorale would open the convention.

Diversity has been an aim of the organization from its inception. Building bridges to communities that might not automatically embrace a predominantly gay men's chorus has been its true focus. TCC has performed with the Male Chorus from the First Baptist Church of Hamilton Park many times (shown narrating at left: Cynthia Dorn). Above right, former Dallas Mayor Ron Kirk joins in the TCC's outreach and TCC members enjoy some back stage time with some folks from Hamilton Park.

My dad turned to me and said he was blessed
to have me as a son that cared enough
to help him open his stubborn eyes....

Dearest TCC: I wanted to thank you for a tremendous gift you gave to me last night. 11 months ago, I decided to come out to my parents (at 37 years old). My dad was recently diagnosed with terminal cancer, and I wanted to be able to stop the hiding and lying to my dad before he leaves us. And I wanted to be honest with him about who I was, so he could love me for who I really am, and not for the lie I was living to him. He had completely stopped talking to me during this time, and I had just about abandoned all hope of ever salvaging our relationship. As fate would have it, my dad and mom were in Dallas for a new cancer treatment for my dad this week. I had heard about the TCC after the Houston pride parade, and the power of healing your music had. So I drove up from Houston, and much to my father's displeasure invited them to dinner and a "concert." My dad had no idea what he was in for (neither did I for that matter). Long story short, in the middle of the Meyerson after the concert, my dad turned to me and said that he didn't care about my orientation, he was just blessed to have me as a son that cared enough to help him open his stubborn eyes. And then I received the first hug from my dad since I came out to him. Thank you TCC for allowing this healing to take place, and providing the setting for the healing to begin within my father's heart. God Bless you all and Merry Christmas!

posted on the TCC website
December 3, 2003

Programming was a small issue. Gary told her, "Chris, you need to trust the process. Tim is a master at programming." And a master bridge-builder, as she was about to find out.

"America the Beautiful," second on the program, had the audience on its feet, screaming. Dr. Seelig now addressed the crowd and took advantage of the goodwill that was still in the air to discuss the Chorale's mission and the need for unity, mentioning AIDS along the way and leaving no doubt that the men in the Chorale were gay. Nothing had been said to this effect prior to this appearance. Most of those present would have been content to think of the group as a bunch of damned fine singers and let it go at that. Left with that impression, however, the Speakers would have remembered the Chorale as a group that had come to entertain them, and bridges aren't built so that the Chorale can provide amusement for people with other things on their minds. Another small success was achieved: new fans for the Chorale's music; an understanding of what the Chorale is singing for, and the likelihood that this understanding would be disseminated, given that the audience was composed of Speakers who would never forget the Chorale's message or the way it was delivered. (In addition, Gary had in effect come out to all his friends in the Association who had had no idea that he was gay. Past President Jeanne Robertson told him, "that was a very courageous thing you did.")

The Chorale isn't wedded to bridges of any particular kind. However, sometimes they are preexisting but unsuspected and all the Chorale has to do is cross or invite someone to join them. Such a bridge enabled them to work with the 100-voice African-American male chorus from the First Baptist Church of Hamilton Park Male Chorus—singing three concert series together over 9 years, making two CD's together and

The TCC and TWCD were invited to perform for the regional convention of the American Choral Directors Association being held in Dallas. In preparation, the chorus 'rehearsed' its concert as a benefit for AIDS Interfaith Network at St. Luke United Community Church, one of the most prominent African-American congregations in Dallas. The convention was being held at the First Baptist Church. The church hosted the entire convention, but refused to allow the one concert featuring TCC and TWCD to be held there. As reported in the Dallas Morning News, the church administrator was quoted as saying "if a convention of adulterers was coming to town, we wouldn't let them sing here." The First United Methodist Church, down the street, graciously opened its doors for the concert in their sanctuary.

TCC sign interpreter Don Jones teaches new members how to sign the Chorale's signature *Silent Night*. Don has signed almost every performance of the TCC since joining as the official interpreter in January of 1989! In 2003, the University of Texas at Dallas/Callier Center for Communication Disorders partnered with the TCC to bring music to its clients and forming the world's first children's chorus for cochlear implant recipients.

even traveling to San Antonio together to give a concert. When some church members got upset at the association of the Baptist choir with the gay men's choir, the pastor of over 50 years said, "We are called to sing, not to judge." That was that.

The possibility of a huge bridge came into existence when the founder of the Susan G. Komen Breast Cancer Foundation, Nancy Brinker, asked Dr. Seelig to commission a massive choral symphony on the stories of breast cancer survivors and the families of those who did not survive. The narrator at the world premiere and on the CD was none other than Dr. Maya Angelou. "Sing for the Cure" has been performed all over the U.S.

Another high-profile success was the "Song of Wisdom from Old Turtle," narrated by Marlo Thomas, created from the beloved children's book by Douglas Wood (who read at the world premiere at the Meyerson in 1999). A portion of recording proceeds benefited St. Jude's Children's Research Hospital. The TCC is also sponsoring the world's only Cochlear Implant Children's Choir.

The essence of bridge-building as practiced by the Chorale is to raise tough questions—and to answer them by doing a program of music instead of handing out attention-getting tracts with closely argued explanations. The men just sing, and through their singing they are making the audience feel good about their country, they're bringing real conviction to their words. And they're forthrightly raising issues that are hard to face involving injustice, misinformation, and the use of fear to smear. Their message is loud and clear, though their voices never need rise above pianissimo.

Longtime hero and singer John Thomas, who passed away from complications from HIV 5 years ago, used to encourage the Chorale to sing and more than that, to tell its story. He was convinced that their singing would change the world. Though they would probably never change those people on the far end of the spectrum of bigotry, there were countless people in the middle who needed to hear their story through music and they would be moved to greater understanding and acceptance.

Perhaps a grudging admiration for the Chorale's singing, or their courage, is all that some members of the audience will feel afterward—still, the chances are good that they won't be hostile. Others will come forward…Some will be recipients of the annual Bridge Builder's Award (established in 2000) for having put their personal reputations or the reputation of their organization on the line to make sure that people know about the bridges they helped to build—and use them. All the Chorale's hard work has been worthwhile when a few people go into a concert thinking, "I don't have much in common with these men," and come away thinking, "They've got courage," for their determination, pride and honesty.

60

The Turtle Creek Chorale has been building bridges around town and around the country. The Denver Gay Men's Chorus welcomes The Turtle Creek Chorale to Denver's Gay Pride Parade. TCC members rubbed elbows with Lily Tomlin after her appearance at GALA in Montreal. The chorale rehearses with the men of Hamilton Park and TCC participates in *Easter In The Park* with the Dallas Symphony Orchestra.

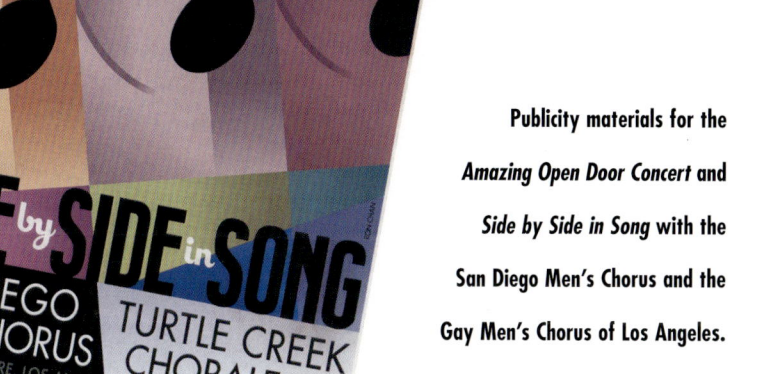

Publicity materials for the *Amazing Open Door Concert* and *Side by Side in Song* with the San Diego Men's Chorus and the Gay Men's Chorus of Los Angeles.

In 2001, the TCC began honoring people who had helped the chorus build bridges to diverse communities. (shown above) Callier Center representatives Kerry and Cheree Noble with their son and cochlear implant recipient, Michael, joined by Dr. Ross Roesser.

(pictured at center) Dallas Morning News columnist Steve Blow and his wife, Lori, and television anchor Mattie Roberts.
(top right) Dr. Seelig, Texas State Representative Harryette Ehrhardt; Office of Cultural Affairs representative Herschel Weisfeld.

(at left) then Dallas Mayor Ron Kirk and his wife, Matrice; Susan G. Komen Breast Cancer Foundation founder, Nancy Brinker; Dr. Seelig; Arts philanthropist representing Dallas's Office of Cultural Affairs, Delores Barzune; Rick Cerillo from American Airlines.

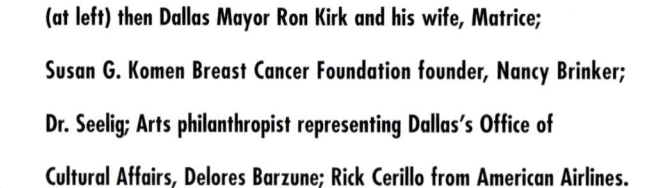

(at right) Receiving the individual Bridge Builder award in 2004 was philanthropist and friend of the TCC, Rex Cumming (center). Presenting the award are art collectors and AIDS activists Cindy and Howard Rachovsky.

THE BRIDGE BUILDER AWARDS were created in 2001 to recognize those who have made significant contributions to the advancement of the Chorale's mission. The Turtle Creek Chorale has spent 25 years building bridges. Sometimes we have built a bridge only to be rejected on the other side. But at other times we have found wonderful partners who have gone out of their way to help us change hearts through the beauty and power of music.

INDIVIDUAL AWARDS

Rex Cumming
Steve Blow
Linkie Cohn
Harryette Ehrhardt
Ron and Matrice Kirk

CORPORATE AWARDS

The Dallas Morning News
Verizon
WFAA / Channel 8
American Airlines

ORGANIZATION AWARDS

Callier Center for Communication Disorders
The Male Chorus from the First Baptist Church, Hamilton Park
Grace United Methodist Church
Susan G. Komen Breast Cancer Foundation

SPECIAL AWARDS

Sammons Center for the Arts, Joanna St. Angelo, Executive Director
Mayor Laura Miller
Black Tie Dinner
Office of Cultural Affairs, City of Dallas

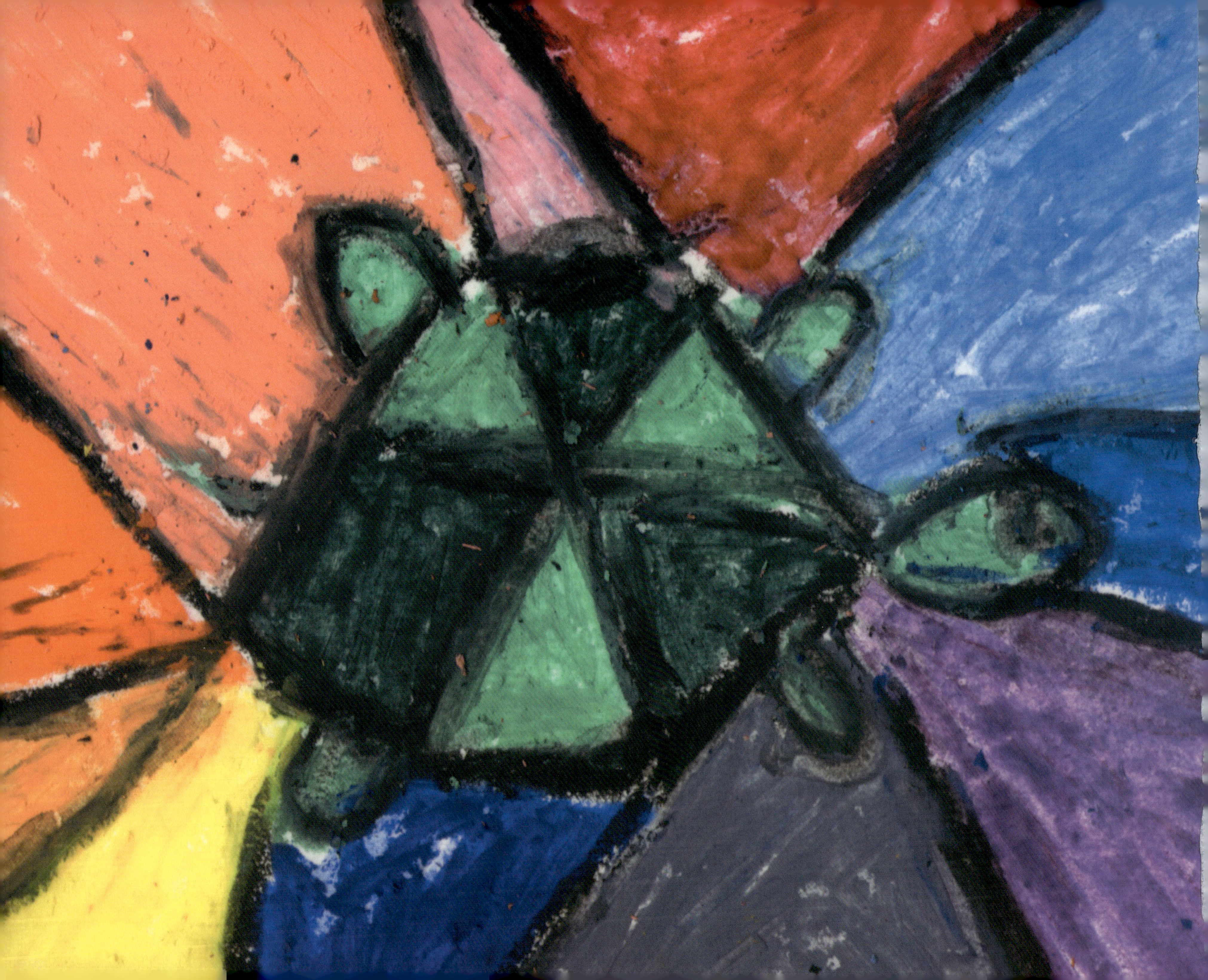

AUDIO TRACK NUMBER NINE

NURTURING
AND RAISING THEIR CHILDREN

Tiny hands reaching, holding, letting go.
    Tiny, tiny feet going nowhere fast.
You cry, can't say why.
We reach, we hold, we don't let go.
We feed, we change, we hold you in our arms and finally…we sing.
Melodious, low, lilting music.
    Not a real song, just a soothing serenade.
Tears of unknown origin cease, our fears disappear as well.
Music has found its mark and done its work.
Tiny hands, much too soon they will let go.
    Tiny feet, too soon they will run away.
And in years to come your tears will spring from deep within.
And when the pain is more than you can bear
    Remember…
    to sing.

Lullaby
Serenade of Life
music: James Granville Eakin III
lyrics: Dr. Timothy Seelig

illustration: Christopher Rattan

NURTURING AND RAISING THEIR CHILDREN

The men in the Chorale with children of their own are generally upbeat about parenting. Among childless members, however, stories like the following are not uncommon. "I babysat my brother's kids a lot when they were growing up. I was their favorite uncle. Then I got a call from my mother on her cellphone from Waco where the youngest was graduating. They said to say hello…I hadn't been invited, you see. That really hurt…"

Many Chorale members have been, at some point, shut out of children's lives—suddenly off limits to teenage nieces and nephews—or told that their own children's friends couldn't spend the night… For the childless men of the Chorale to have children of their own is almost more than they dare hope for: more than for straight parents, it can be a matter of money and luck.

Adoption is expensive. Chorale members Mark Hayward and Richard Galvan had to pay a set fee of thirty thousand dollars to an adoption agency in Guatemala before they could come away with their infant son Christian (now well known to Chorale members from Tuesday night rehearsals; many of Christian's new uncles have held him in their arms). "The paperwork was incredible," says Mark. "Thirty pounds of paper. Christian only weighs twenty pounds right now."

Christian has been a delight: a healthy, curious child…who has never once wakened in the night since he found his new home. He is being raised hearing lots of music: Richard at the piano or playing the violin, Mark on cello. Veronica, a Spanish speaker who helps care for Christian during the day, says that the boy is particularly attentive to Richard's piano playing. He understands her Spanish, but when she goes home at night his fathers tell him, "No more Spanish now. Spanish is going bye-bye." The loving home these men are providing for Christian is satisfying in yet another way: Mark was abandoned by his parents at age 18, Richard's parents abused him. "We take special pride in being able to give Christian an upbringing unlike ours," says Mark.

Rob Lynch and his son Evan are pioneers. Evan was 5 weeks old when Rob adopted him. Evan is a mixed-race child, and acceptance by their neighbors in Richardson (Canyon Creek) was a concern, but they are doing well there. In a recent epiphany, Rob saw that his primary interests in life at this time more closely resemble those of a typical heterosexual couple: soccer, the PTA, cub scouts… Cub scouts was hard for him, but he saw that his feelings about the organization were standing in Evan's way and he relented. This isn't the first time he let Evan find his own way: at 2 years Evan was left with Hamilton Park daycare to resolve some behavioral issues that may

There was a time when children were not a part of the TCC. The members enjoyed children only as nieces and nephews or as children in a classroom. This has changed drastically as we are now privileged to do everything from sharing the stage with them to adopting our own.

One of the courageous dad's in the TCC is first tenor David Jenkins. David and his partner (TCC member Bruce Carter) are now helping raise David's triplets. David is associate professor of social work at TCU, where he has taught since 1991. He also maintains a part-time private practice for therapy in Fort Worth, Texas.

Who would have thought when this gay men's chorus was formed 25 years ago that they would ever need child care? Well, TCC Child Care is here. Pictured are dads and kids with their Tuesday night 'mom' Sharon Lammers.

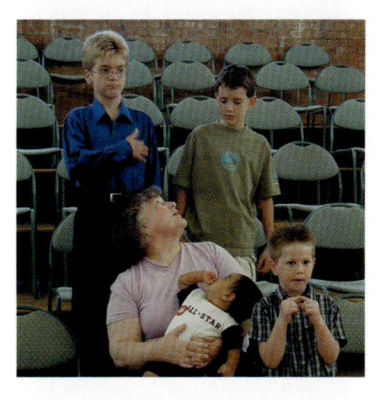

have been identity-related. Evan comes to nearly all the rehearsals; he knows the Sammons Center better than the men in the Chorale. Sharon Lammers (TCC Associate Member) has cared for him there and obviously adores him. Rob feels that the Chorale's fellowship is an important reason that Evan is so outgoing and personable. Brian Larrison's son Ethan, now 5, is following the trail that Rob has blazed. It leads to the front lines for gay parents everywhere: soccer team and cub scout meetings, and school activities, where their parenting skills are closely scrutinized. Rob has not only survived, he's made some allies. He points out that more than any child in any other family, a child adopted by a gay parent knows he is wanted.

What special qualifications might the men of the Chorale bring to fatherhood? An ability to sing an effective lullaby or a rollicking "Old MacDonald's Farm"? Perhaps, but some members have inadvertently revealed what kind of parents they might be, the kind of nurturing they might provide. Working with the Callier Center for Communication Disorders, the Chorale has engaged in a life-changing, if not world-changing experiment: the world's first choir for cochlear implant children. Chorale members Reed Hoke and Sam Bass conducted the first complete session of classes. With 15 years of public school music teaching between them, they brought energy and patience to their work. Says Reed: "In the first sessions last year we tossed a pen in the air to show the high voice and growled like bears for them to understand the low. Now we use a koosh ball…It's more fun for them." Parent Sara Tranchina had this to say: "Emily really looks forward to coming to choir practice! The enthusiasm of Sam and Reed is contagious, and to see our kids smiling and to hear them singing is a real treat…I can see real progress."

After a painful separation from his wife more than seven years ago, college professor David Jenkins has developed a close relationship with his daughters—triplets!—described in a recent article in Evolve Magazine. Jenkins teaches social work at Texas Christian University and is a family therapist as well. He believes he is a more compassionate therapist for having been through all the twists and turns of coming out. He feels a great camaraderie with all the other dads in the Chorale, and needs their support: it's hard to balance parenting with his job and his other responsibilities. "Last night I was on the way to the Chorale when I got a call on my cellphone. 'Dad, did we have a soccer meeting?' I turned around. I have missed a fair amount of rehearsals because of soccer games. With three girls the same age, everything has to be super-structured: everything comes to a stop for them." Yet the rewards are tremendous and his partner Bruce is beginning the foster child/adoption process… David's girls have had problems having their friends spend the night, but in general they're well-adjusted and enjoy coming to concerts of the Chorale. "These are the ones who can imagine a just society," says David of them proudly.

When Dr. Seelig came out and took the position offered by the TCC his children were 7 and 9 years old. They immediately had over 100 uncles added to their family. Over the last 18 years, the men of the TCC have kept close watch on the conductor's offspring. Through Tim they have lived with the ups and downs of parenting and being a gay dad. All members with children, either biological or adopted, are assisted in countless ways by their fellow members of the TCC, from baby-sitting to entertaining, to parental advice from those who don't have kids (sometimes the best kind). Tim's children specifically had many hands helping them and holding them, but especially Louis, Shawn, Robert, Kenn, Anne, Trigger, Eve and Carol. Tim is pictured here with daughter Corianna. She is a pediatric oncology nurse. Tim's son is a C.P.A.

Joe Rattan had this to say of relations with son Chris. "He is just approaching an age to understand about me. I am trying to create a place for him where fear is not a part of the equation. I want him to question, discuss and discover his world, and be fearless in living his life." Joe also adds, "I am introducing him to wonderful, loving people, so that he has a frame of reference. If there comes a time when people say somthing hateful about me or other gay people, I can respond positively by asking him if that sounds right based on what he knows to be true—rather than responding in kind—with hate and ignorance."

Tim Blanchard-Modisette has helped raise partner Pat's three children for the last seven and a half years. From the beginning, the children were very accepting. When Tim and Pat had a formal union in 1998, all the boys actually participated. It was a traditional wedding with three hundred guests; the boys lit the candles. The kids go to all the Chorale's concerts. "When we're going to do something we always ask them, do you feel comfortable going? We tell them, 'This is how we'd like you to participate, but you don't have to.' They've never refused. They always end up going."

Kirk Bradford's Kali wants to make use of the expertise she's gained from her association with Chorale members who have pored over wedding catalogs with her. When Kirk came home from rehearsal recently, she told him, "Dad, you know, I'll never have to worry about my wedding. I'll never have to worry about flowers, dresses, anything…"

The men of the Turtle Creek Chorale continue to nurture their families. Of course the men are devoted sons and brothers and uncles. But many are dads and even granddads. And yes, they have pictures in their wallets!

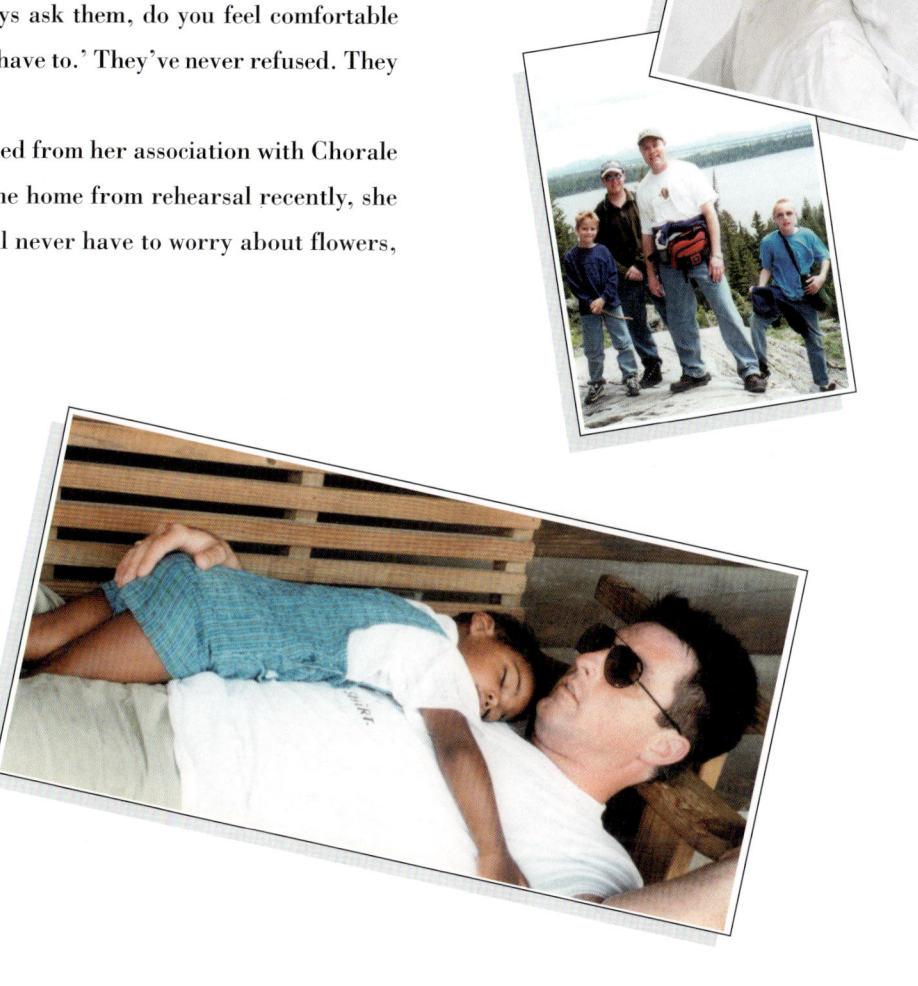

When the time came to record the work, the logical choice to read the narration was a woman who had spent her life working for the care of children: Marlo Thomas. She read the book, listened to the music and said an unqualified "Yes!" to the invitation.

For several years, members had suggested to Dr. Seelig that he read the award-winning book *Old Turtle* by Douglas Wood. At the time Tim said he already knew enough old Turtles. Finally, a staff member gave him a copy. The words lit a fire under him and Tim began to negotiate with the publishers of the book to set the text to music. They were not so sure, but after two years of persistence, they finally agreed. Composer Joseph Martin (*The Awakening*) set the book to stunning music worthy of the beautiful message and breathtaking watercolors in the original. It was the first time the Chorale had commissioned a work that specifically spoke to children, although the book certainly has an adult message as well. Joseph Martin set it for narrator, orchestra and chorus. At the world premier, parents got in free with a child and each child was given a book as a gift so that they and their parents could read along as the choruses sang. As the 1,000 people in the hall read along, many of the children sitting in their parents' laps, those in the audience said it sounded like angels' wings when all the children would turn the page at the same time.

YOU ARE OUR SON

Jason Walker

You are our son.
No matter what others may say,
You were our son from the moment
    you were born.
God made you for us and us for you.

We loved you before we knew you.
You were what our hearts ached for
Before we realized our hearts were aching.
You are and will ever be what makes us family.

You are our son.
No matter where your dreams take you
Home will always be where you come to rest.
Home will always be where you soothe your soul.

When your plans fail and your heart breaks;
When friends turn away and your faith shakes
We will be there to listen and comfort.
We will be your champions
    when you've fought all you can.

When you have reached the pinnacle of success;
When the world knows your name
    and craves your glance
We will know you best and love you most.
We will love you not for what you've done
    but who you are.

You are our son.
When you find the love of your life
    and the joy of your heart
We will celebrate with you and love them
    as our own.
We will teach you what we have learned;
Love is about who and not so much why or how.

When your love brings you
    the ecstasy you bring us
We will bless your new family with the gift
    of our family.
We will look on with care and concern
    offering wisdom when asked.
We will allow you to learn from your mistakes
    and missteps.

Our prayer for you is that God will give you…
Happiness so you can laugh,
Strength so you can endure,
Imagination so you can dream big,
Courage so you can do much,
Compassion so you can heal,
Openness so you can learn,
Wisdom so you can teach,
And love so you can live.

As you grow and learn,
As you dream and yearn,
As you rest your head and close your eyes,
Do not fear when doubts arise.
This one thing you can know for sure,
You are our son.
You are loved.

photo: DVC Photography Dallas, TX

The poem on the preceding page was written for Richard Galvan and Mark Hayward to honor the arrival of their son, Christian. The pictures to the left of the poem were taken in Guatemala during the adoption process: a long and complicated "labor" that was well worth both men's unstinting commitment of money, time and energy. Richard Galvan is shown (left) holding his pride and joy for the first time. At this point the paperwork to formalize Christian's adoption greatly outweighed him!

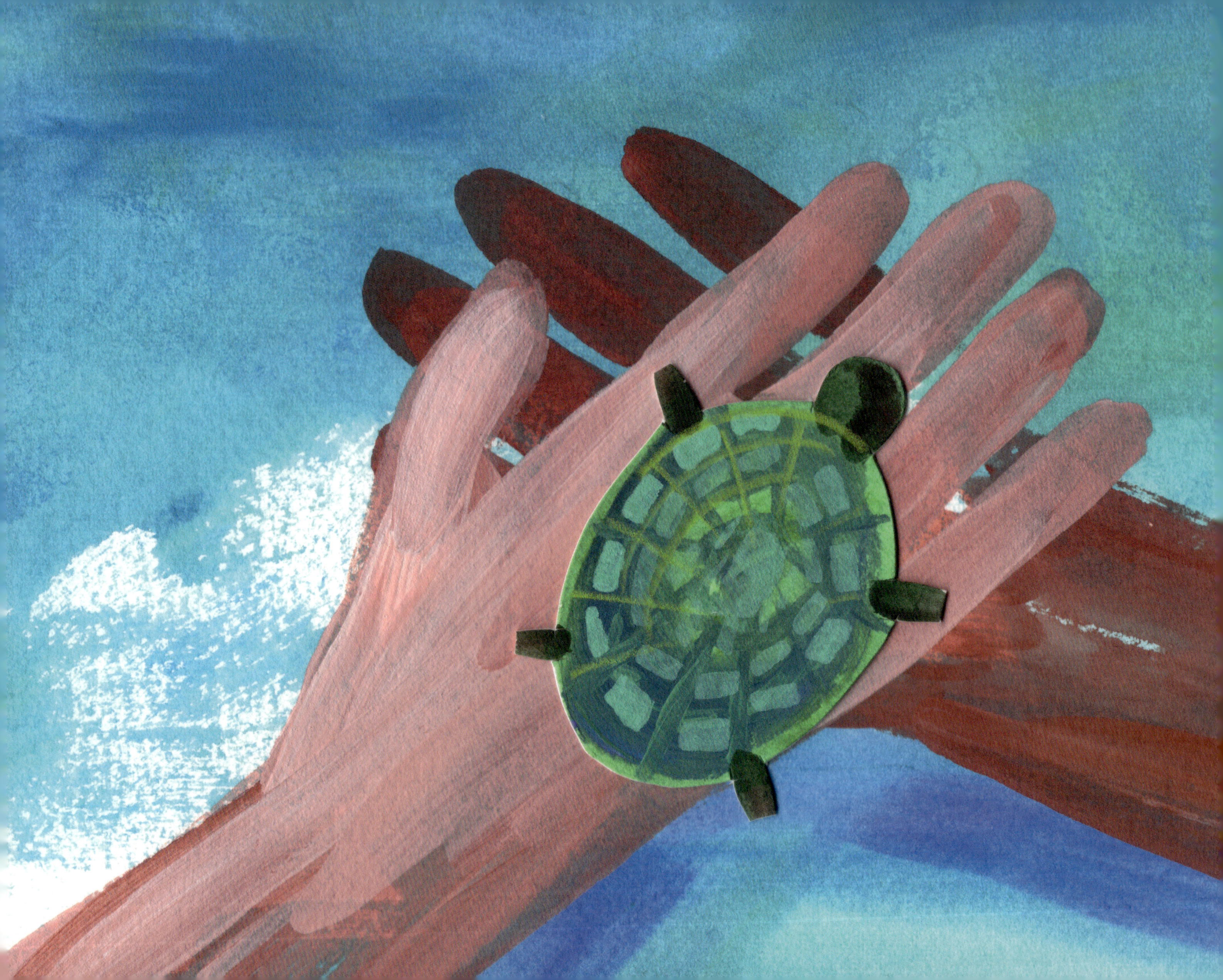

AUDIO TRACK NUMBER TEN

Sharing
THEIR LIVES WITH EACH OTHER

I've got a roof over my head. I've got a warm place to sleep.
Some nights I lie awake counting gifts instead of counting sheep.

I've got a heart that can hold love. I've got a mind that can think.
There may be times when I lose the light and let my spirit sink.

But I can't stay depressed. When I remember how I'm blessed.
Grateful, grateful, truly grateful I am.
Oh Grateful, grateful, truly blessed and duly grateful.

In a city of strangers, I've got a fam'ly of friends.
No matter what rocks and brambles fill the way,
I know that they will stay until the end.

I feel a hand holding my hand. It's not a hand you can see.
But on the road (of Life) to the promised land, This hand will shepherd me.

Through delight and despair, Holding tight and always there.
Grateful, grateful, truly grateful I am.
Oh Grateful, grateful, truly blessed and duly grateful.

Grateful
music & lyrics: John Bucchino

illustration: Joseph Rattan

SHARING THEIR LIVES WITH EACH OTHER

Sharing music with the world is the first goal of the TCC. But sharing each other's lives runs a close second. It happens in rehearsals, in performances, on tours and just about everywhere two or more are gathered.

Before they ever open their mouths to sing a note in rehearsal, new members are introduced to one important way the Chorale practices sharing. They will be paired off with a big buddy as they come through the door: a project that is unofficially in the hands of a senior member (such as Keith Wall). The new member will sit with his big buddy and learn everything he needs to know about the singer-conductor relationship here at the TCC, about how rehearsals are conducted, and what it means when the conductor conducts himself a certain way. The big buddy system is one of the first ways the Chorale starts fulfilling its role as the singer's surrogate family: for example, Keith Wall is Rob Nichols's big buddy, and they've called each other "big brother" and "little brother" for five years. As it happens, Rob lost on older brother who was two weeks apart from Keith in age...As he would have with his big brother if he were alive, Rob shares the ups and downs in his life: his career, his love life, his artistic aspirations, as well as the kind of day or week he's been having, and of course Keith shares all the same things with Rob.

The importance of sharing comes across inadvertently in what Reed Hoke says about his big buddy, Gary Williams. When Reed came to Dallas from Indianapolis more than 10 years ago, he was a little intimidated by its size and the size of the Chorale. "At my first Chorale rehearsal, I was so nervous I appeared to be standing in one place, 'cruising' Turtles. Anyway, that was the gist of Gary's comment to me. Since he had spoken to me and had 'baritone' on his name tag, I latched on to him and said, 'I'm sitting next to you!' (I had been singing baritone in Indy.) A couple weeks later Gary became my big buddy (because, unbeknownst to me, he'd asked to be). I was touched by his friendship and support and we sat together, non-stop, for four years. After I moved away and came back to Dallas, we needed first tenors. I was a tenor in college, so I volunteered to move up. I was as sad to leave Gary's side as he was to see me go, but we make it a point to say hello and give each other a kiss and a hug at every rehearsal and performance." Needless to say, in more commercially oriented choruses, tenors sing tenor, baritones sing baritone—or they don't sing. And Reed wasn't pulling the wool over Tim Seelig's eyes: he's Tim's assistant and now works full time for the Chorale.

Members of the Chorale stay in touch and their homes are often used for quasi-official celebrations (a pool party to reward the bass section for selling the most raffle tickets at the recent auction, for example). Members' homes are more than way stations for a moveable feast: children are being raised in some of them,

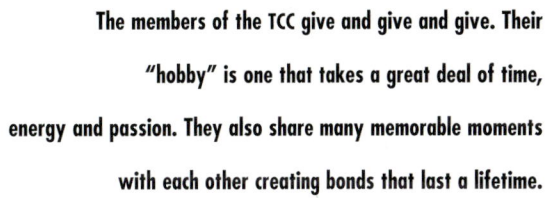

The members of the TCC give and give and give. Their "hobby" is one that takes a great deal of time, energy and passion. They also share many memorable moments with each other creating bonds that last a lifetime.

In 1992, the TCC performed for the national touring AIDS benefit show called Heartstrings. Backstage, while waiting to perform, they shared the hall with an African-American male chorus from the First Baptist Church of Hamilton Park. Thinking it a long shot, Dr. Seelig asked their conductor, John Tatum, if they would ever sing with the TCC in a concert. The answer was "Yes." Thus began a long relationship between the two choruses that resulted in three series of concerts spread over the next ten years, two CDs and an appearance together at the Texas Choral Directors Association state convention in San Antonio. At first glance, these two choruses shouldn't actually work together. But through the power of harmony and commitment to music, they became one.

The Turtle Creek Chorale is my family because it accepts me for who and what I am... it is always there for me to come home to.

For two years now, I have wanted to stand up at the end of retreat and say something, but I just never had the courage. So I thought about writing this letter. Because of events in my life over the past few months, I feel as though I really must do this.

So much was said Sunday about how important the Chorale is to everyone, about how it fulfills so many needs, about what it means to be a part of this "family." Well, I concur with everything that was said. You all ARE my family; not because all of my friends are in the Chorale--they aren't; not because my boyfriend is in the Chorale-- he isn't; and not because my life revolves around the Chorale--it doesn't. The Turtle Creek Chorale is my family because it accepts me for who and what I am and supports that. The Chorale is my family because it is always there for me to come home to. I'm very lucky to have close relationships with a mother and sister who accept me and the fact that I'm gay, but they are in Tennessee. When I joined the Chorale, I found a family close to home, and I thank all of you for that.

a letter written by a member
to the Turtle Creek Chorale
February 6, 1995

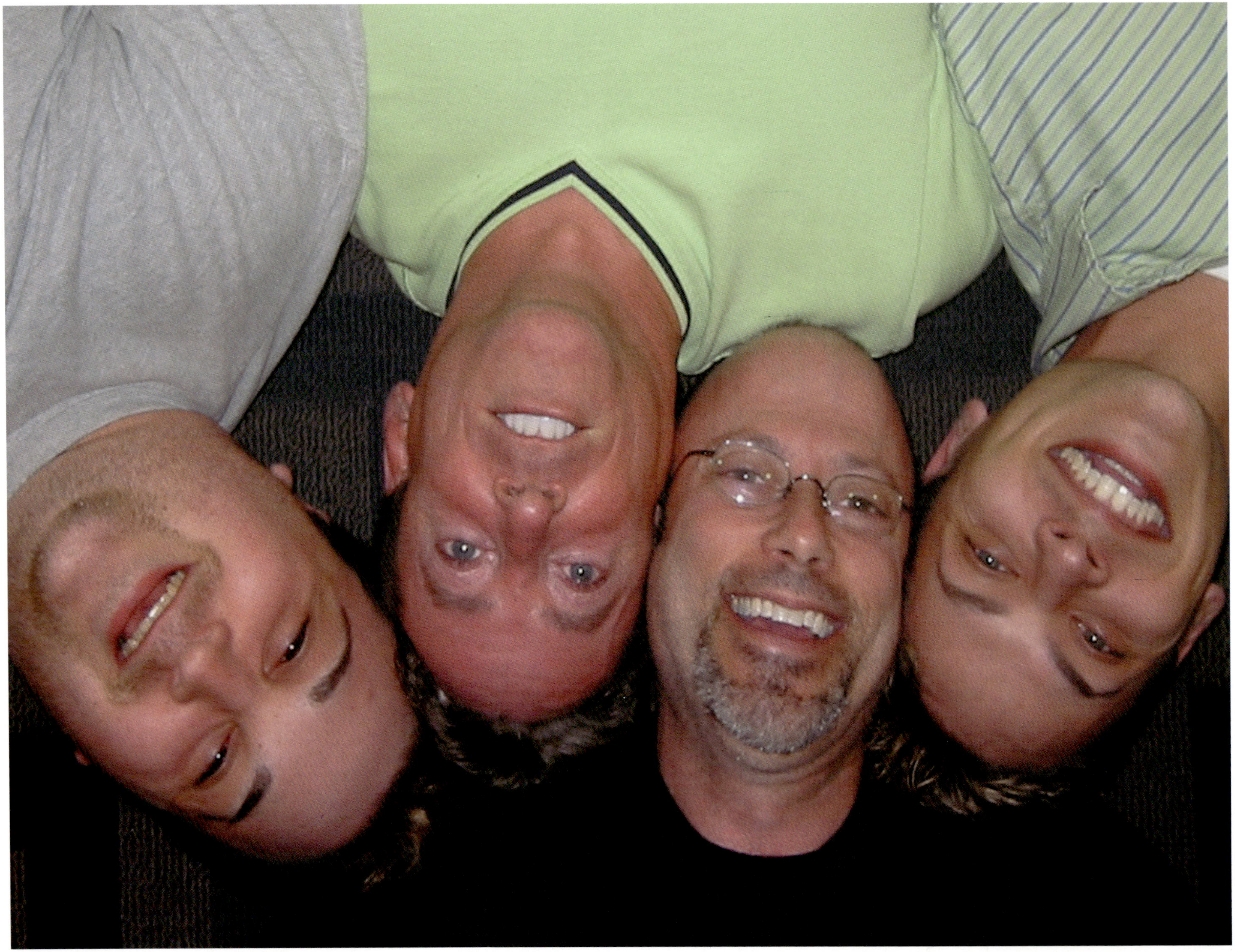

such as Christian, the little boy adopted in Guatemala by Mark Hayward and Richard Galvan (a delightful distraction at recent Tuesday night rehearsals). As Kali Bradford put it (when she was 11), "I bet I have more uncles than any kid in school." And there will be more than one of them on the phone to her father Kirk to ask if he can take her shopping for school supplies. Another favorite "date" with Kali is gay bingo, where she's a regular (and earns spending money by charging the men who sit with her for cuss words at 50 cents per. Some give her as much as twenty dollars on account at the start of the evening.)

It's apparent that the men who are big buddies to each other are uncles to the children in each other's lives. It is not just an extended but an extending family—extending a helping hand in a host of ways, extending a commitment of time or effort or cash beyond what merely shows concern, "to let you know we care." Concern for each other is intrinsic to all their relationships as it might be instinctively for blood relatives. Nor does it flow in only one direction, from the Chorale to people who need their help. Sharing has a passive aspect as well, in that Chorale members need to be gracious guests as well as gracious hosts, worthy recipients of love as well as unstinting givers—accepting the love of another member's mother, for example.

Some mothers and fathers will travel great distances to hear the Chorale. Over the seventeen years of his membership, Scott Davidson's mother was well known to hundreds of members, and went from Georgia to Carnegie Hall to hear them sing. Near the end of her life, she took a notion to visit Hot Springs, Arkansas for Thanksgiving. Scott moved her there while she was on oxygen, with her IV running, only to lose her the day before the holiday. He was hit with an outpouring of e-mails and letters of condolence from the Chorale before he left the resort. But the Chorale goes beyond pro forma expressions of support and sympathy by distilling a tribute from their emotions laced with talent and energy: by singing. If the parents who have become fans will travel great distances to hear them, Chorale members will travel great distances to sing at funerals, commitment ceremonies, weddings. When Scott lost his partner of 11 years, for example, A.G. Black traveled more than a hundred miles to the little Texas town where services were being held to sing at his funeral. The author of "Serenade of Life," James Eakin, will never forget the way the choir turned out to sing at his wedding here in Dallas. The way the Chorale has "sung for the cure" is described elsewhere, but of course what they are doing

How do they do it? It's not always easy. The chorus members give their all. Not only do they 'volunteer' their time (they actually all pay dues to be a part)—they also pay for their wardrobe and all travel. But it is their belief that together they can do more to change the world than they ever could as individuals that keeps them coming back and giving and giving.

is sharing of the highest order: sharing of their message of hope, sharing of their commitment and courage—raising their voices to confront those who have the means but not the will to ease the suffering of great numbers of citizens, male and female, or even to end it. While our society is still afflicted by dread diseases like AIDS and breast cancer, these men and the women who now sing with them will continue to afflict the consciences of the willfully ignorant with poignant beauty and frank urgency: if they can be made to weep, perhaps they can be made to think.

If sharing has a serious side (everything the Chorale does has a serious side) it can be fun, too. At retreats (twice a year) there's a Sunday meeting that has become a high point for many members. The retreats in Texoma take place in cabins beside the lake, though there is a hall with a piano to accommodate all the singers (usually about a hundred and fifty members attend). After rehearsing Friday night, all day Saturday and singing in a No-Talent Show on Saturday night, members are partied out by Sunday morning and for some reason are more inclined to open up at this time than any other. With the sense that nothing, nothing can destroy their feeling of family unity, the men "share" (in the therapeutic sense) their deepest doubts and fears, as well as their appreciation of each other as a source of love and laughter. Upon returning to their homes late Sunday, many members describe a sense of healing and renewal. This feeling carries over to sectional rehearsals that take place on the average every other Sunday. Discussions that began in the open atmosphere of retreat then deepen, and of course there is always more to share because even in the closest families trust is given in increments and doors open slowly and never all at once.

In order to know each other better and ensure that each member is a presence in other members' lives, about ten minutes before each performance Director Seelig assembles the Chorale and asks them to name anyone special who will be attending the performance: relatives from out of town, coworkers. This probably increases the level of performance anxiety (not necessarily a bad thing if Seelig can convince the men they're better than they think, as he routinely does in performance by communicating his trust in them) but it has a deeper meaning and more lasting effect. The men are reminded that they're not merely musicians or performers who are about to go onstage and do what they do best. They are meant not to forget who they are as people, as individuals. Nor is the audience meant to become a black abstraction out beyond the footlights: even if they can't be seen, its members will be thought of, as the men sing, as members of the Chorale family. Thus, they are not a room full of critics whose approval is being sought, they are about to be included in the sharing and receive the men's gratitude for being there.

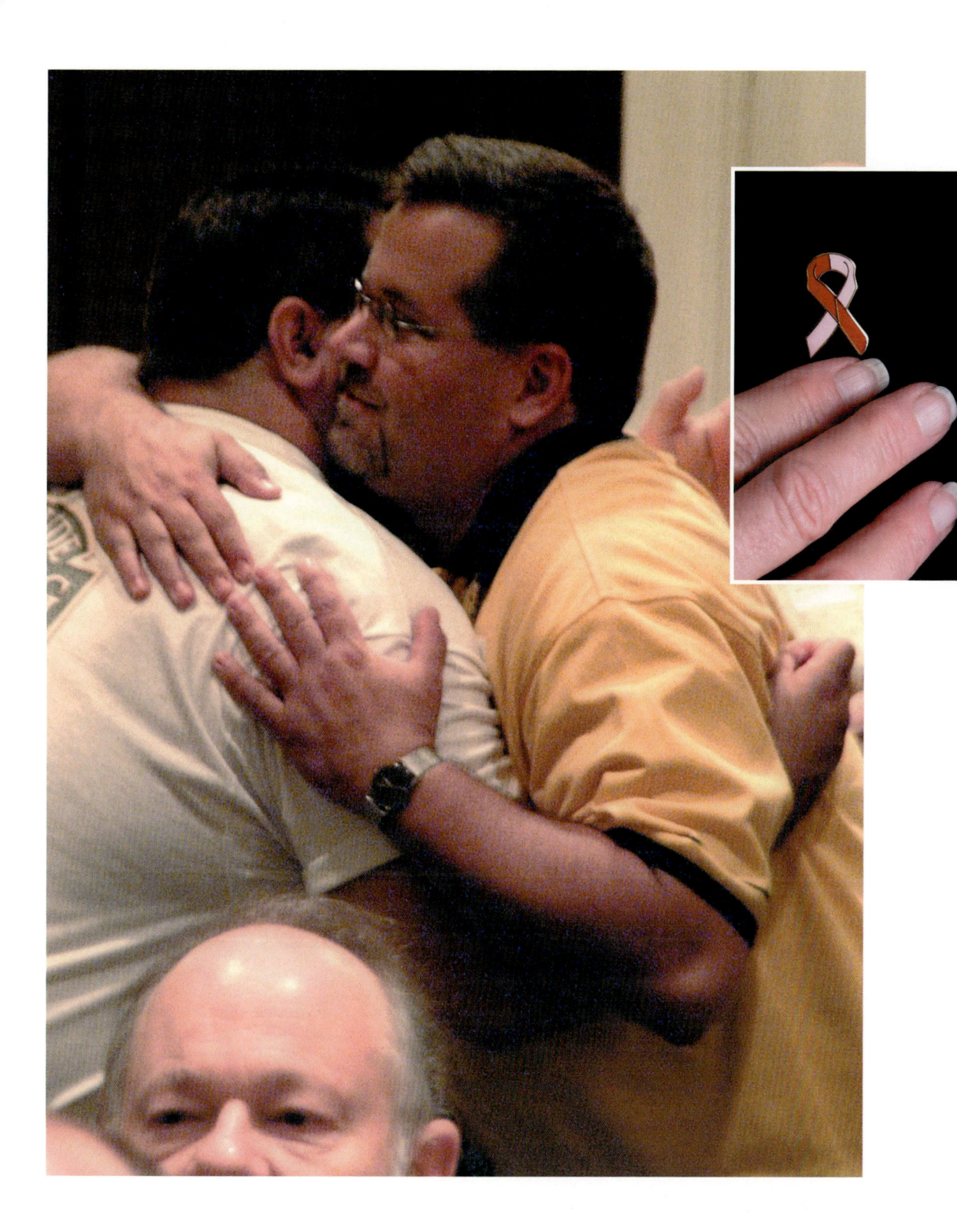

The sharing of the now red and pink ribbon has become a symbol of unity and awareness for the TCC. We have shared the "pinning" with friends both far and near. New members of the TCC are "pinned" backstage by their big buddy before their first on-stage performance with the chorale.

It is not particularly unusual for singers in the TCC to find the love of their life and make a commitment. It is more unusual for TCC members to meet each other through the chorus and remain members. It is still another level of uniqueness to have two singing members decide to have a public holy union, invite TCC members to perform and have one of the men's three children participate in the ceremony. This is the story of Tim Blanchard and Pat Modisette (pictured at far left), who decided to proclaim their love for each other in a very traditional church ceremony, accompanied by Pat's three children. They even took each other's names as Tim and Pat Blanchard-Modisette.

Almost from the beginning, the chorus went out of town to have a weekend retreat to learn music and strengthen the bond of brotherhood. Pictured is an out-of-town retreat at Lake Murray, Oklahoma. What is retreat? A time to share our "innermost" selves. That may be frightening, but everyone gets to be whoever they want. For whatever reason, this often results in people dressing up as women who really should not and who never would at home. Only at a state lodge in the backwoods of Oklahoma would they truly feel pretty.

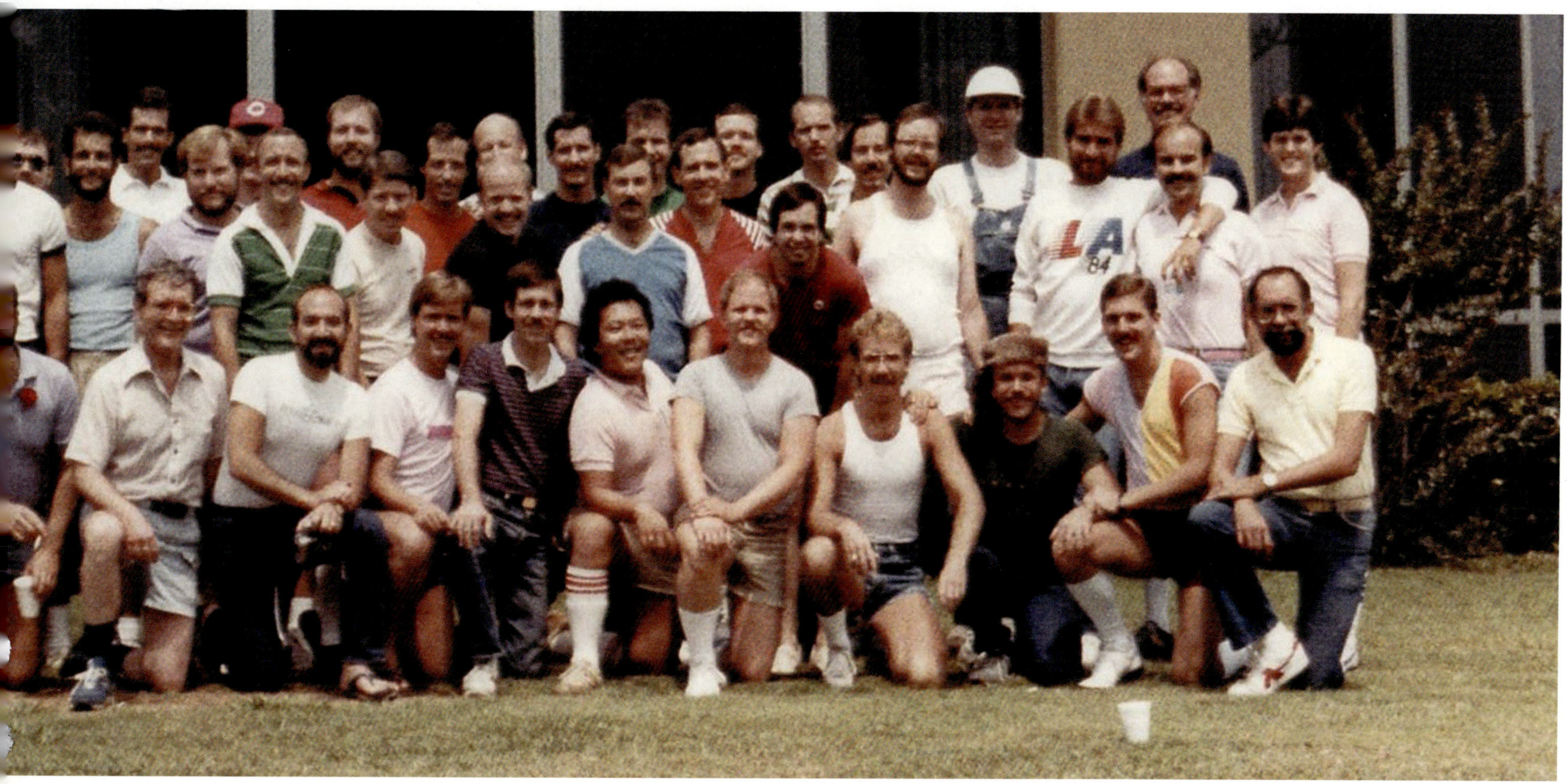
LA
84

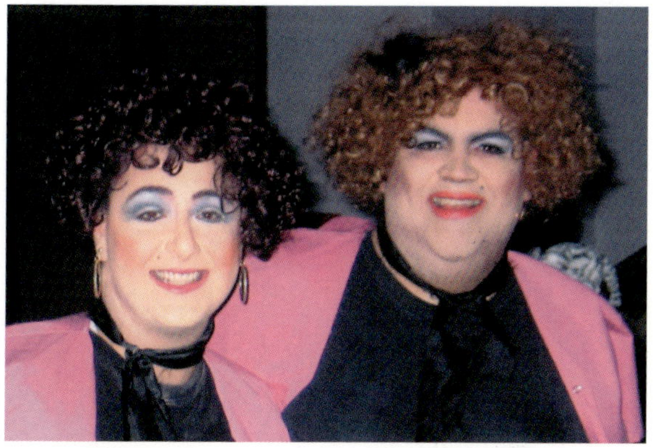

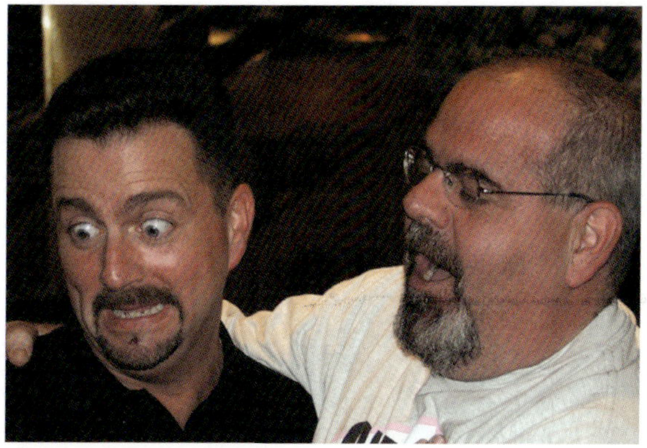

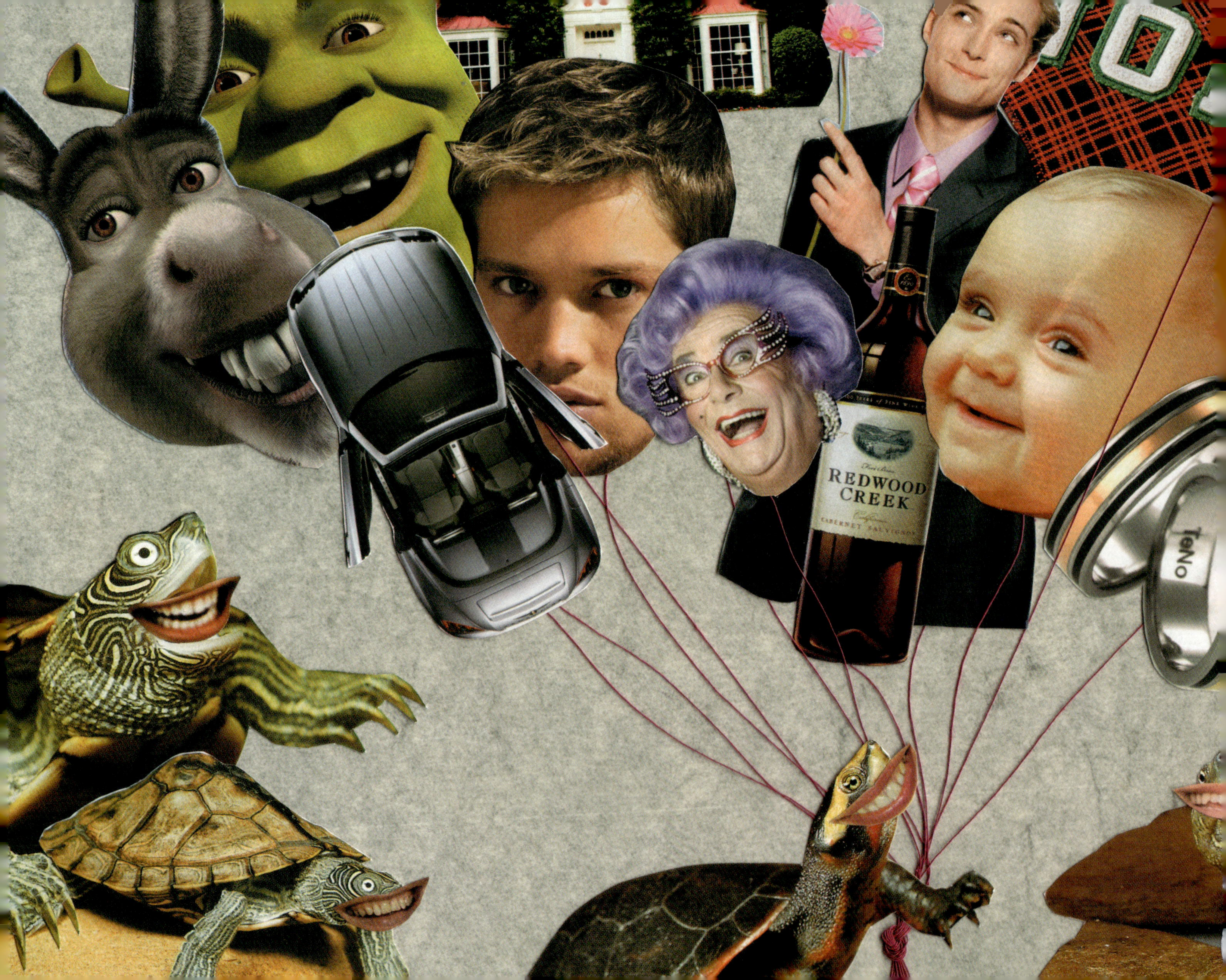
REDWOOD
CREEK
CABERNET SAUVIGNON
TeNo

AUDIO TRACK NUMBER ELEVEN

Celebrating
SIGNIFICANT MOMENTS

Can't hear you knockin'
there at my door
Can't hear your footsteps
across my floor
See your lips movin'
can't hear a sound
Too busy livin'
livin' out loud.

I'm not defeated
you have not won
Race is not over
just startin' to run
Givin' you notice
time you saw the light
I won't surrender
decided to fight.

Life is a feast
and I'm here to dine
eat every mouthful
drink all my wine
I'm at the table
you can't take my plate
I'm slammin' the door
and lockin' the gate.

Don't be mistaken
don't be deceived
Leave when I'm ready
come when I please
And when I go
my head won't be bowed
Go like I came here
livin' out loud
Go like I came here
livin' out loud.

Livin' Out Loud Blues
music: Robert Seeley
lyrics: Pamela Martin

illustration: Joseph Rattan

89

CELEBRATING SIGNIFICANT MOMENTS

The Turtle Creek Chorale gets together to celebrate almost as much as it gets together to sing, and sometimes the men celebrate by singing, so it's hard to say where one begins and the other leaves off.

They celebrate by singing when they sing "Happy Birthday" to each other, which because of the size of the group happens frequently after rehearsals. Thus, each member of this large family gets to be center-stage at least once a year.

For a majority of members, each year's holiday celebration is the most eagerly awaited. Christmas might be a sad time for men alone or separated from their biological families, but the Chorale keeps its singers busy. Its Christmas programs usually feature original music and choreographed festivities. The Poinsettia Tribute is a chance to remember departed colleagues for all they gave to the Chorale. In essence, the members who carry on the tradition are reminding themselves that the most important gift they have to give is the gift of themselves, the gift of time and interest to the rest of the group, the gift of attention and encouragement, the gift of hard work and God-given talent. This giving is continuous. It is taking place every day of the year, and it is never forgotten. The Chorale couldn't be more like a family than it is now (for some men, the only family they know), celebrating the contributions of all of its members, even those who have gone on.

As soon as they join the Chorale, members get to know each other by celebrating. First year members attend an orientation celebration each year at someone's house where they enjoy food, drink and games. It's not all fun, though. Last year members watched *After Goodbye* and heard from officers of the Chorale about what to expect and what would be expected of them. So there was a celebration and an orientation and new members were shown the dual aspect of family life in the Chorale. The Chorale is deadly serious about its mission, and its mission is never forgotten. It is the ultimate meaning of everything the Chorale is trying to accomplish. At the same time the Chorale is a resource for its members. Sometimes it's even a refuge. Members who have been going through a bitter divorce, who have been estranged from their children or rejected by their parents have special emotional needs and the Chorale tries to meet them.

Celebrations frequently set the stage for emotional breakthroughs. Cecil Sinclair acknowledges that he had walled off his personal life after an unhappy relationship years ago, and in addition his father hadn't spoken to him for five years. "Still, life is okay…The music makes it okay." After a holiday concert

Lucky Queen.
Dr. Seelig meets Queen Elizabeth II as the TCC performs for her visit to Dallas in 1991.

According to founding members who still sing, from the first note of the first song, Randall Thompson's *The Last Words of David*, the TCC sound was magic. One of the early successes was TCC's appearance at the Johnny Mann choral festival where they met their 3rd conductor, Michael Crawford. In the early years, Caruth Auditorium at Southern Methodist University was the perfect fit for the TCC size and sound. As the Chorale outgrew and shed that shell, it was most fortunate to be able to make the glorious Morton H. Meyerson Symphony Center its new home in 1994.

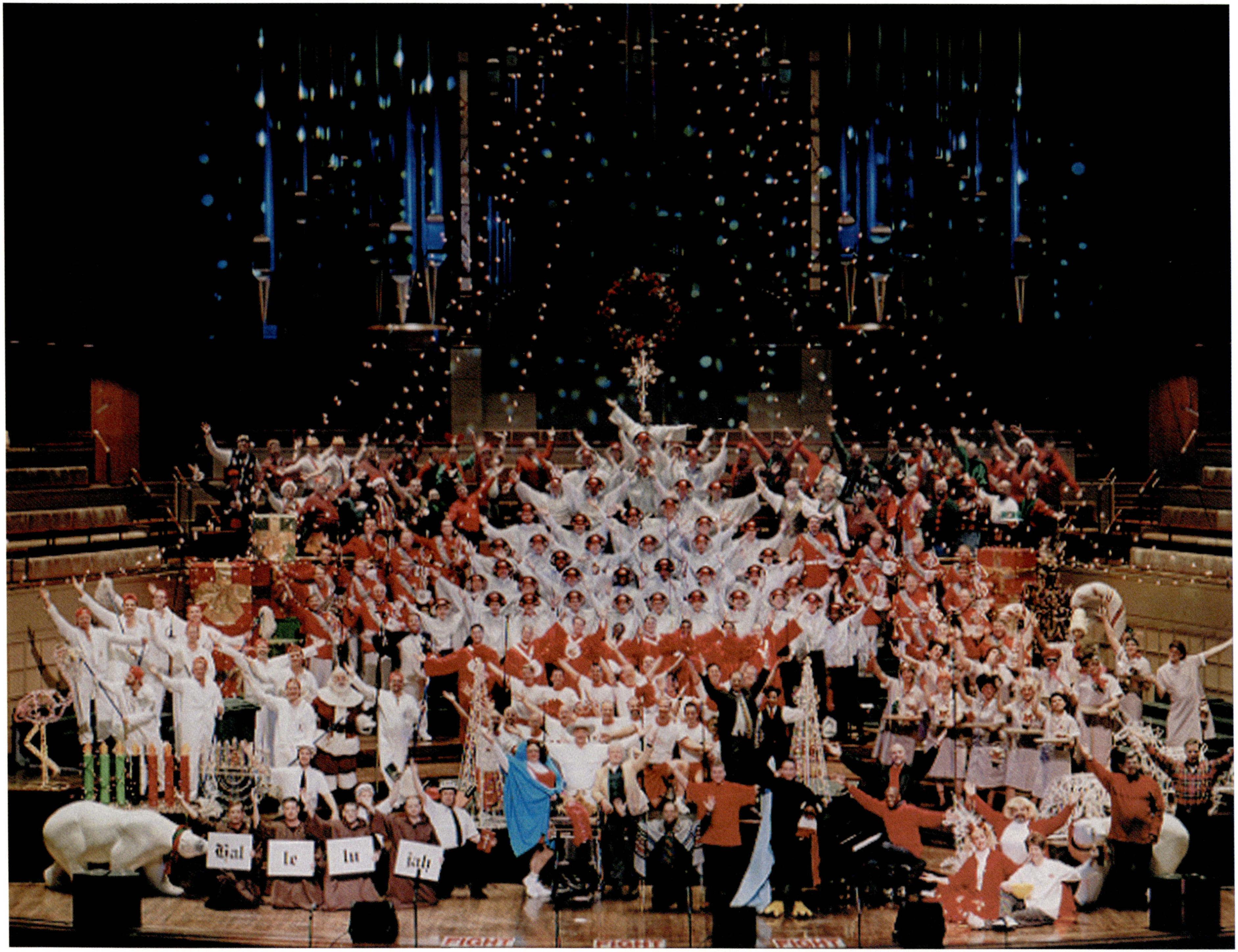
Hal
le
lu
jah

In the evolution of the chorus, not only did the sound continue to mature and stun listeners, but the productions, especially at the holidays, became more elaborate and outrageous, pushing the capabilities of the symphony hall to the limit. Shown on the previous page is the holiday concert from 2001. It included a marching band, Luby's waitresses, cheerleaders and a Living Christmas Tree spoof... all from within the chorus.

with the Chorale his father showed up unexpectedly and invited him home to Christmas dinner. "That's when I realized the power of the Chorale."

The celebration itself is enough sometimes, designed as a simple ritual that can spin off into the private lives of members. For example the Chorale celebrates with its supporters in the audience when the men leave the stage en masse after singing "Silent Night." Each member stops, when the music stops, to touch the member of the audience who is nearest at that moment. Completely by chance, Michael Brantley found himself standing next to his father when the music stopped. As matters stood, his father had told Michael that he didn't approve of his lifestyle but he still loved him. There had been an emotional estrangement from his parents from the time Michael was a kid in Alabama. Michael put his hand on his father's shoulder and, looking down, noticed that he was crying. This was more than Michael could take. Though he was his father's son, and not given to tears himself, he began crying also and subsequently Michael and his father embraced and erased the distance that had grown between them.

At celebrations, Chorale members who know each other as fellow musicians start to know each other as people. News of personal upheavals is never out of bounds. Members don't have to "make nice." Members don't have delicate ears. Celebrating is a way of surmounting problems that would tend to fester in isolation. Getting together with other members after the breakup of a relationship is an example. Instead of bemoaning all that he's lost, the member can celebrate his newfound freedom, and hoist a glass in gratitude for the friends from the Chorale who are sticking by him.

This year's GALA convention in Montreal was pretty much a nonstop celebration, but the first celebrations took place before the Chorale left. Excellent hors d'oeuvres and drinks were provided gratis at the Dralion restaurant as a send-off. In fact, parties with food and drinks are a favorite way of rewarding each other. This year the bass section sold the most raffle tickets for the auction and were rewarded with a pool party...

Celebrations aren't always planned and some of the spontaneous ones are most memorable. At the last Christmas concert at the Anatole Hotel, there wasn't room on the stage for all the poinsettias to be hoisted in tribute. The first year class improvised, making stars which bore the name of a departed member. The stars were then held aloft instead of a poinsettia at the right moment. Everyone in the audience understood exactly what was happening and why.

93

Among the best-loved celebrations have to be the times the Chorale itself is being celebrated. It's one thing to be thanked by local charities and told how well you've done by people who've become familiar faces in the audience. And it's quite another to be told by one gay chorus after another, as the TCC was told in Montreal, that you're the best they've every heard, you're an inspiration, you set the standard, you really do make a sound like none other on earth. Many members heard remarks like this. There were other comments that speak to an evolution in the Chorale's public persona. Joe Rattan reports that he was told by members of other choruses that the TCC should be congratulated for its friendliness and openness, especially since going in it had a reputation for being a little aloof, a little patronizing. Apparently much more than respect was won this time around.

The Chorale makes a gift of its music to raise money for important causes and its members make a gift of their time and talent to the Chorale. It is from this carefully crafted political structure that all blessings flow. Though it's easy to take the political organization of the Chorale for granted, imagine for a moment what might have been. Suppose that soloists from the Chorale were paid, or paid on a sliding scale, according to their seniority (as with a professional, union chorus) or paid according to the importance of their parts? It's not hard to imagine how jealousy and dissension might arise.

With the TCC, celebrations are never investitures. Good news about any member is always welcome but celebrations are reserved for the victories the men have achieved working together. They belong to all, from the first speech down to the last dessert.

Celebrating important moments within the chorus is a highlight and natural outgrowth of spending so much time together. Whether a milestone birthday party, a pajama party at retreat, or celebrating with friends such as former Texas Governor Ann Richards, life in the TCC is joyous.

In one wonderful and memorable evening, I received the magical gifts of laugher, thought and tears as my heart and soul were touched....

Could a simple "Thank you" ever suffice for the wonderful gifts which I received last night, when I had the great pleasure of attending your Holiday Concert? I do not think so. This was the first performance of the Turtle Creek Chorale that I have had the opportunity of attending. I can assure you that it will most definitely not be the last!

I made my living as an actor and entertainer for twelve years, and I will tell you that out of all the Christmas shows that I have ever seen—both live and televised, your concert was the most creative, original and heartwarming. I still have waves of emotion hit me when I think back on the performance. From the beginning to the end, I was completely enthralled. In one wonderful and memorable evening, I received the magical gifts of laughter, thought and tears as my heart and soul were touched. Your love and sincerity for what you do shines brilliantly to all who are observing.

Thank you, thank you, thank you again. I know that I will continue to say thank you in my heart until I have the pleasure of seeing TCC again.

a letter to the Chorale
posted to the guestbook
December 9, 2003

96

TCC Elves and the NBA! Did that actually say Turtle Creek Chorale and National Basketball Association in the same sentence? Sure did. Yes, it's true. Thanks to TCC member and choreographer Shawn Northcutt's position as one of the Mav's ManiAAcs, the TCC wangled an invitation to appear on court at half time of one of the Dallas Maverick's basketball games. The crowd of 18,000 went wild for a hundred or so elves "taking the court."

98

It was Dallas resident Charles Hodnet and his partner Tony who took Houston resident Tim Seelig to his first TCC concert while he was visiting Dallas one weekend. After Tim applied for and got the job as Artistic Director, moved to Dallas and was living next door to Charles and Tony, he asked Charles if he had ever thought of dressing up as Santa Claus. The rest is history. Charles has been a fixture at TCC holiday concerts ever since and has become one of Dallas's most famous Santas. His tenure rivals Don Jones's 16 years as signer.

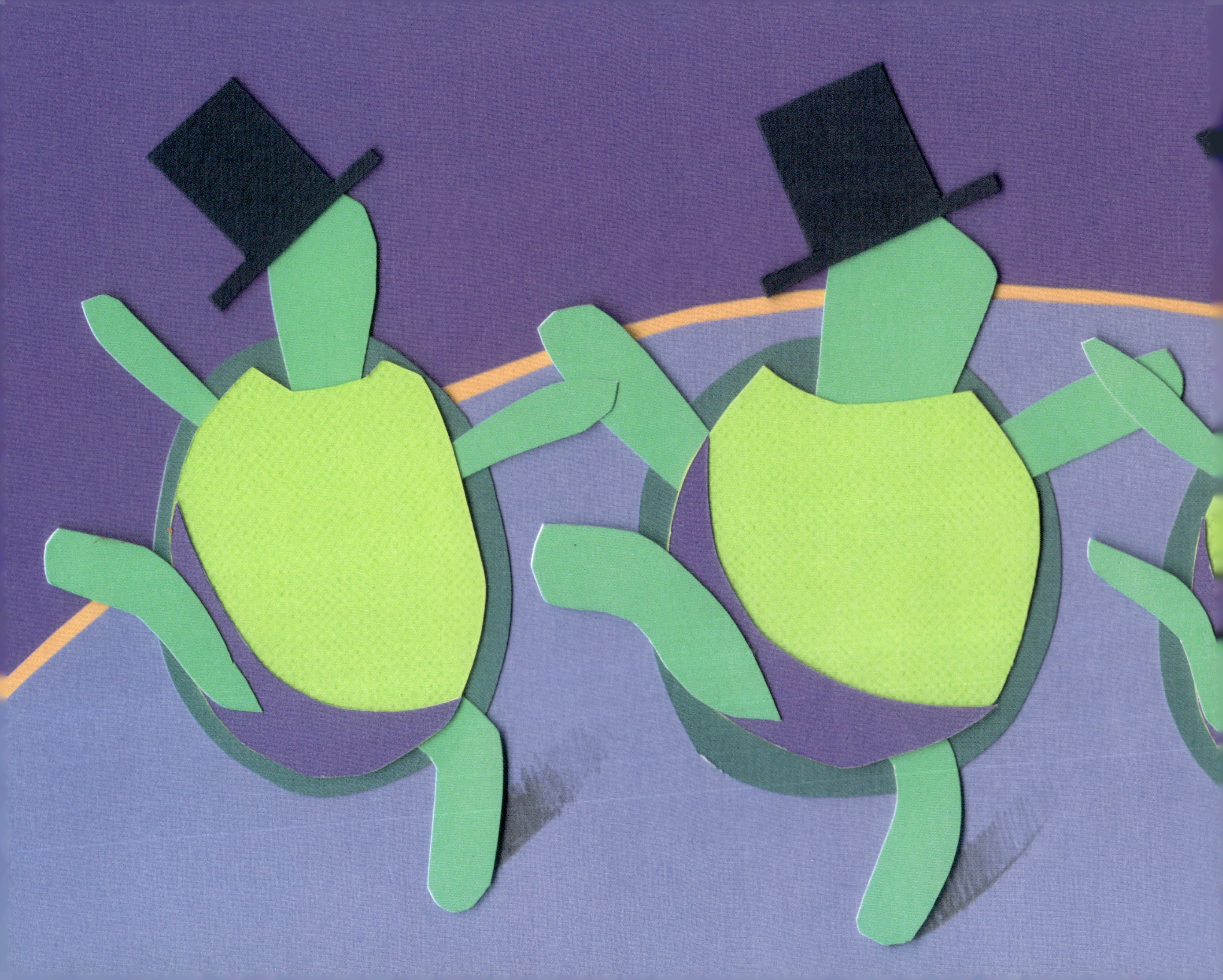

AUDIO TRACK NUMBER TWELVE

Laughing
AT THEMSELVES AND THEIR WORLD

Lord, won't you help me? It's that time of year. Winter has come and gone, summer is here. In this season of flesh, won't you show that you care? Lord, won't you hear this dieter's prayer?

Teach me tonight, to love cottage cheese, grapefruit and celery,
Lord, if you please. Make him believe that tofu's a food
And not something you made up, when you were in a bad mood.

Lord won't you help me? Show that you care.
Oh, Lord, won't you heed this dieter's prayer

Keep him away from the refrigerator door. When life is a trial and love is a bore.
Oh save me from nachos and tacos and chips.
'Cause what goes in my mouth always lands on my hips.

Oh, Lord can you hear us? Honk if you're there.
Oh, Lord, won't you heed. You know my need.
Lord won't you heed this hungry and desperate dieter's prayer?

Dieter's Prayer
music: Gerald Sternbach
lyrics: Amanda McBroom

illustration: Joseph Rattan

101

LAUGHING AT THEMSELVES AND THEIR WORLD

At some rehearsals, there seems to be as much laughing as singing. The laughter starts at the podium, where Tim is having a good time, then rolls through the room. The men leave their bad mood from work at the door and the great thing is that many of them don't pick it up on the way out.

What's so funny? These men were once the butt of jokes about "girlie men." Trying to escape these hurtful jokes many withdrew and tried to fit in by living a lie. Some joined in the jokes to avoid suspicion. Then after years of painful self-awareness, they refused to live that way anymore.

Many Chorale members learned to sing in church or school choirs, some were even music majors in college, but few were able to experience the truth of who they were along with the passion they felt for music. This happens joyously at their first Chorale rehearsal when they will almost certainly laugh or cry, finally able to do what they love with people who love and accept them completely. This joy overflows the room even before the music starts. Then the singing begins, the voices of 200 men creating what Tim Seelig calls "a blanket of you. You are whole at that moment."

So the fun begins with the knowledge that whatever happens they will no longer be skewered by a malicious intent lurking behind a façade of business as usual. Tim departs from the script by putting malice first and making it ridiculous, or launching innuendos that fly harmlessly by without stinging. "Girls, what are you thinking about singing that way?" he may chide the basses. When the sonority of the chorus leaves something to be desired, Tim may tell them: "That's the nelliest sound I've heard since the Texas Girls Choir sang last year." Terms like nelly and butch are put to good use to describe the singing as well as to characterize members' lives outside the chorus by laughing at the world's perception of gays in general. There will be jokes about relationships, weight, age, everything in between—high taste, low taste and no taste. The first tenors are the divas. The basses are the foundation of the chorus when they're not out having a cigarette. The second tenors are really first tenors with too much testosterone. The baritones are underachievers with pretty voices.

Using these terms once hurled at them about each other, there is an opportunity to help the audience to experience the same self-awareness and acceptance. For the men, there's the chance to achieve something even more: some self-respect, incredibly hard to achieve when gay persons are so often portrayed in the media as second-class citizens and sinners.

Given the task of creating glasses to wear for the concert of Elton John music, each TCC member was given a pair of large plastic glasses to decorate. The results were beyond what Sir Elton ever wore.

The Award Winning
TCC Strangerettes
2002

The Kilgore Rangerettes are a Texas tradition. One of the TCC members, Gary Williams, set about creating a group from singing members to rival that troupe, naming it The Turtle Creek Strangerettes. Pictured here in front of Dallas City Hall, the group has now won awards in Dallas and Houston and is international, having performed in Montreal, Canada. Watch out!—they may be coming to a city near you soon.

103

104

Always pushing the envelope on the zany, especially at the holidays, Dr. Seelig felt it was most appropriate that the chorus give homage to one of the holiday's battle-scarred warhorses, The Nutcracker. But, not being able to find 200 tutus that would actually fit around the guys' waists, they went on their heads! At right is another tongue in cheek send-up, this time a group of monks using cards to 'sign' the Hallelujah Chorus.

TCC retreats have long been known for the Saturday night "No Talent Show." At one such extravaganza, singing member A.G. Black appeared as Miss Big Thickette, performing a rousing *Stars and Stripes Forever* while hammering nails into a sawhorse. Convinced that people back in Dallas needed to see such talent, the retreat show was repeated at home as an AIDS benefit. Thus began a long line of title holders (or sash queens) who throughout the years spent their time and energy to help raise money for the TCC AIDS Fund. It is the one title in Dallas that can be bought. You raise the most money for the AIDS Fund, you win. Each title holder has brought his/her own unique talents to the position and together they have raised tens of thousands of dollars for the cause.

Teaching, too, is done from the podium with humor. The shoulder massage to begin rehearsal is a David Letterman monologue. Warm-ups are physical and fun. Even when a singer blurts out a wrong note at the wrong time, there is goodhearted laughter, but the men aren't laughing at the offender, they're laughing with him.

No one's religion is off limits, by the way. Besides members of local gay congregations there are Methodists, Jews, agnostics and undecideds. The altar boys get a large share of the jabs, followed by the Southern Baptists and the Pentecostals.

Poking fun isn't the only way the men laugh, however. Because they know each other's stories, they can share joyous moments when the Chorale connects with its audience. Board member Doug Frankel recounts a sublime moment at Carnegie Hall when partner David Daigle's relatives, sitting in the front row, leapt to their feet to applaud David in particular upon his entrance. This attention might have embarrassed someone else but his friends in the Chorale knew enough of the story to laugh joyously—not the laughter of ridicule that needs to be stifled but the kind that stays in the heart and warms it. (The story is classic: David's parents were immigrants from Canada who just made it across the border to Ft. Kent, Maine, where David grew up. Carnegie Hall represented a dream come true for their son.)

The comedy most identified with the Chorale is, of course, the sort called "camp." Imagine the last holiday concert with two hundred men in tuxes, twelve flutes, a harp. Strains of the Nutcracker begin and before the audience even knows what has happened, all two hundred have tutus on their heads and have literally become the Waltz of the Flowers. Or imagine the concert of the year before last with two hundred elves. Then there was the time they did synchronized swimming. They dove behind blue fabric and when they came up, all two hundred had on pink bathing caps for the rest of their routine.

The chorus might be as famous for their camp routines as for their sound. Years ago, at the infamous Esther's Follies on 6th Street in Austin, Dr. Seelig saw "Patsy Cline" sing "I've Got Your Picture" while pulling props out of her dress. It began with a picture but then there was a princess phone, records, a bra, and she finished with a full-size saw, golf club and crutch. The audience was on the floor. Tim asked the woman to come to Dallas,

There are not many musicals that can be performed with an entirely male cast (plus one girl). But in 1993, the TCC decided to tackle a huge production of none other than *The Wizard of Oz*. The production turned out to be a perfect fit for the Chorale and was repeated in 1997 with the cast pictured below right. Above that picture, Paul Williams, who played the wicked witch in both productions, rides in the Alan Ross Freedom Parade as the WW herself.

and she did, but the Chorale couldn't afford to take her on tour, so one of the men learned it, in full drag, and mastered the timing. Patsy went on tour to Europe with the TCC and appeared at the national ACDA convention in San Diego. By now, she has toured most of the GALA choruses around the country.

In the upcoming season, there will be a return of the Ballerhinos, the "big girls" who will dance as Sugar Plum Fairies. And A.G. Black (originator of the Miss Big Thickette beauty pageant) will bring back the latest version of Mrs. Santa, who has given up her lounge act to start a dot.com. A.G. has been a mainstay of the Chorale's comedy over seventeen years of membership. His creation of Cindi Claus trying to perfect her lounge act ("the frozen North can be such a drag with all those elves and Santa wanting all the attention") has set the standard for Eskimo chic. ("In her first incarnation, under her pinafore she was wearing gold lamé Capri pants with a red tulle hostess skirt.") A.G.'s apotheosis comes about when he delivers his Christmas medley, a near 12-minute muddle of 64 Christmas carols (with "Somewhere Over the Rainbow" thrown in), precisely musical, with quarter-tone deviations from pitch where necessary. She can't keep "Frosty the Snowman" distinct from "Rudolf the Red-nosed Reindeer," even though the reindeer in question and his mincing consort are both on rollerskates. After Cindi Claus is finished, so is her audience, or if there are any survivors, they've been changed for life.

Through the years, there have been the Barbeque Boys with a precision lawn chair routine, the monks or nuns under a vow of silence who must "card" the Hallelujah Chorus (the year the holiday show was country-themed they sang the "Jalapeño Chorus"), the stripping hiphop Santas… Then there was the time Carmen Miranda's hat was wheeled on looking like a tray on a fruit cart…and Carmen uncoiled out of the cart and did a routine with the inflatable banana boys. Through it all, Dr. Seelig banters with the audience, trying to make everyone comfortable, even if they don't want to be.

Some 12 years ago, a group from the Chorale formed a faux drill team on the order of the Kilgore Rangerettes. They called themselves the Turtle Creek Strangerettes and performed for a Halloween parade. They performed at the Houston Gay Pride Parade in 2003, and won the two top trophies. In 2004, they took Montreal by storm and in July of 2005, will conquer the granddaddy of them all, the San Francisco Gay Pride Parade. They aren't all pretty, but they have huge hair and they sure can kick. In addition, like Mrs. Santa and other stalwarts of Chorale comedy, they take their art very, very seriously.

One never knows where the TCC will end up on tour, or who they might meet! Whether in the historic halls of Europe or posing in front of one of a chain of convenience stores in Mason City, Iowa. The sublime or the ridiculous?

109

110

Dancing snow men, roller-blading reindeer, monks "carding" the hallelujah chorus so that they won't break their vow of silence! You never know what holiday tradition the Turtle Creek Chorale will lay bare. Mom may be developing a crush on Santa. Mrs. Claus, also known as Cindi, is looking to bust out of the north pole to go on tour. But laughter isn't the only dimension to a TCC holiday concert. One patron remarked, "I feel every emotion in a Chorale concert that I feel during the holidays—the laughter, the joy, the tears and the memories are all there...it's my favorite part of the holiday season!" Many feel that their holiday celebration begins with the Chorale's first holiday performance.

It was the middle of November. The TCC was filming its 2nd holiday television special at a brand new performing arts center (the Eisemann Center in Plano, Texas). There was only so much time to film because of the hall and because of costs involved. The chorus was all dressed as elves, the band was ready, the stage set, when fire alarms began to sound. Everyone was evacuated from the building while the fire department was called to make sure everything was OK. So the elves headed for the streets, armed only with emergency provisions: cigarettes and cellphones.

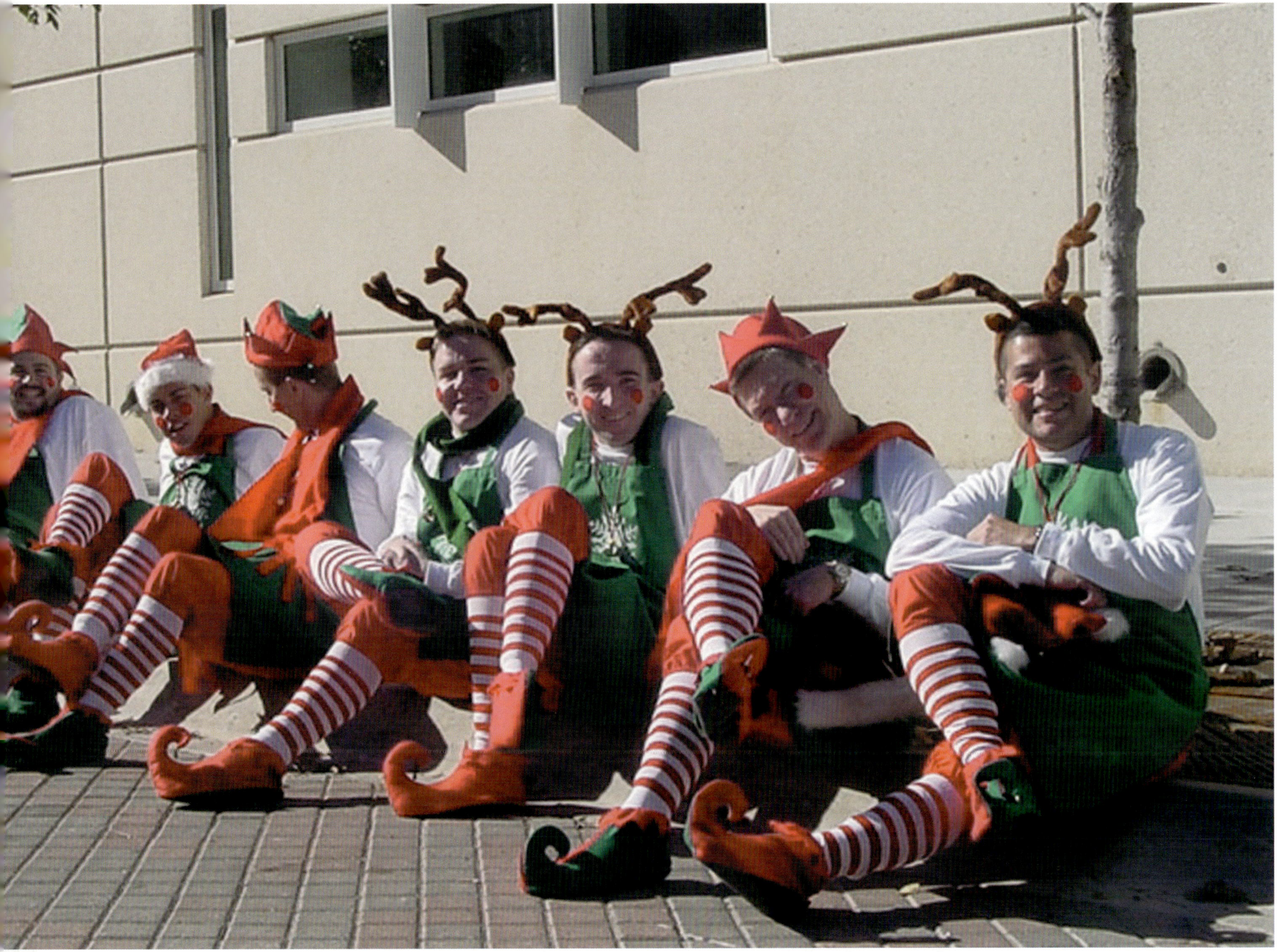

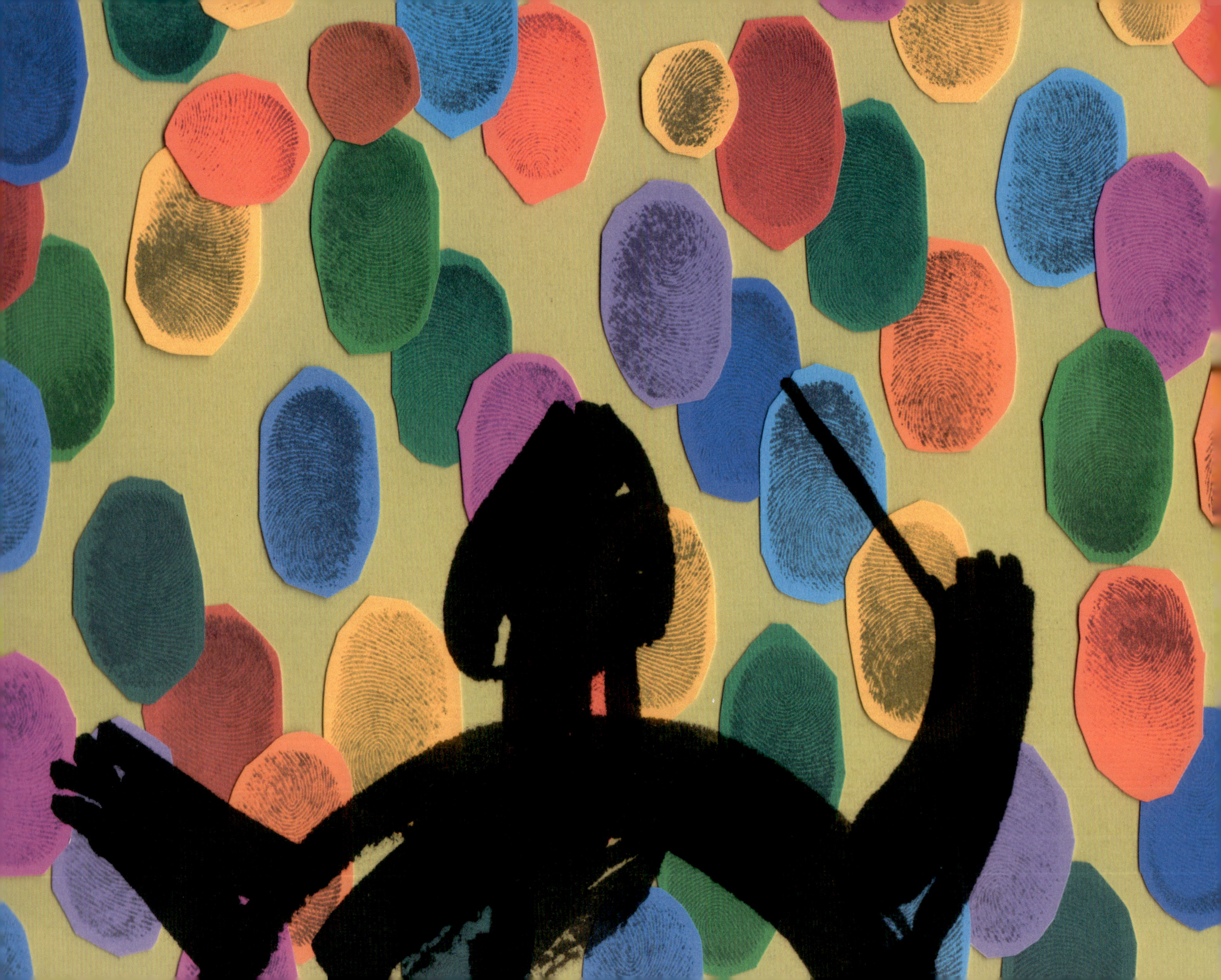

AUDIO TRACK NUMBER THIRTEEN

BONUS AUDIO TRACK NUMBER FOURTEEN
I Ain't Afraid
music & lyrics: Holly Near; arranged: Steve Milloy

LEADING
THEIR COMMUNITY INTO THE FUTURE

Something inside so strong
The higher you build your barriers the taller I become.
The farther you take my rights away the faster I will run.
You can deny me, you can decide to turn your face away
No matter cause there's

(chorus) Something inside so strong
I know that I can make it tho' you're doin' me wrong, so wrong
Thought that my pride was gone, oh no
There's something inside so strong. Whoa oh
There's something inside so strong.

The more you refuse to hear my voice the louder I will sing
You hide behind walls of Jericho your lies will come tumbling.
Deny my place in time you squander wealth that's mine
My light will shine so brightly it will blind you
Because there's (chorus)

Brother and sisters when they insist we're just not good enough
Tho' we know better just look 'em in the eyes and say
We're gonna do it anyway, we're gonna do it anyway
We're gonna do it anyway, anyway. (chorus)

Something Inside So Strong
music & lyrics: Labi Sassri

illustration: Joseph Rattan

115

LEADING THEIR COMMUNITY INTO THE FUTURE

The Chorale has become what it is and remains what it is because Dr. Timothy G. Seelig realized who he was, chose to tell the truth about it and to remain that person. And because he's someone who wants to have fun, and for those he works with to be having fun. ("If rehearsal's not fun, the men won't keep coming back.") He's not an autocrat like most conductors. He doesn't use his authority to keep his singers at a fearful or respectful distance. He's a friend to these men, a father or a brother, and his door is always open. Their personal growth is more important to him than their growth as musicians.

Unlike nearly all other conductors, Seelig is a great singer who doesn't sing. When he sang a season with the prestigious St. Gallen Opera (Switzerland) after training at the Mozarteum (Salzburg), Seelig was turned off by the egocentric lifestyle demanded of a full-time opera singer. It was opera's loss: his voice is unforced, warm, and full of things to say (like Fischer-Diskau's). In revolt against the forcing of voices to characterize, and as a connoisseur of voice quality, Tim favors untrained voices that reveal what's inside over voices that have been trained to sound dark and metallic, always, no matter what the singer is really feeling.

Unlike other conductors—and most people—Seelig places no dollar value on his exertions commensurate with his growing fame. His value to the chorale is incalculable, but the Chorale is a non-profit [501(c)(3)], the singers are volunteers. Leading by example once again Seelig never grubs for money, nor has he ever cut back and tried to give less of himself. A vacation for Tim means that he comes to work in cutoffs and goes barefoot.

As for the personal qualities that make him the ideal musical and administrative director of the Chorale, Managing Director David Mitchell is incisive: "He engages people…he's so engaging. He's really a good speaker, he makes people laugh. A wonderful businessman, you know…unusual in someone with so much artistic talent. A diplomat, an executive…And he's great at fundraising."

Tim himself explains the success of the Chorale as a kind of divine accident. The Chorale doesn't have an executive director as a check on the artistic director because "I fight these battles within myself before I go to the board for money," Tim says. When the board is unable to give him money for a project he believes deeply in, he raises the money personally. (Such projects have made significant returns for investors, though some, like member Scott Davidson, have reinvested their earnings in the Chorale.)

Chorale administration doesn't exist to say no to Tim Seelig. In any case, most of them work for him in his capacity as chief operating officer (according to Mitchell, this is still Tim's role, although at some point

Bad dress rehearsal, great performance. After an especially grueling rehearsal, longtime Director of Artistic Operations, Craig Gregory, tells the truth to Tim. Not always a pretty sight.

From day one, the TCC was blessed with an abundance of talent on the podium. The first three conductors are pictured at the right: Harry Scher 1980-1981; Richard Fleming 1981-1983; and Michael Crawford 1983-1987. All three laid a foundation that would serve the TCC far into the future.

Arriving at the TCC in 1987 with hair and no gray in his beard, the youthful Tim Seelig has never lost his young-at-heart spirit.

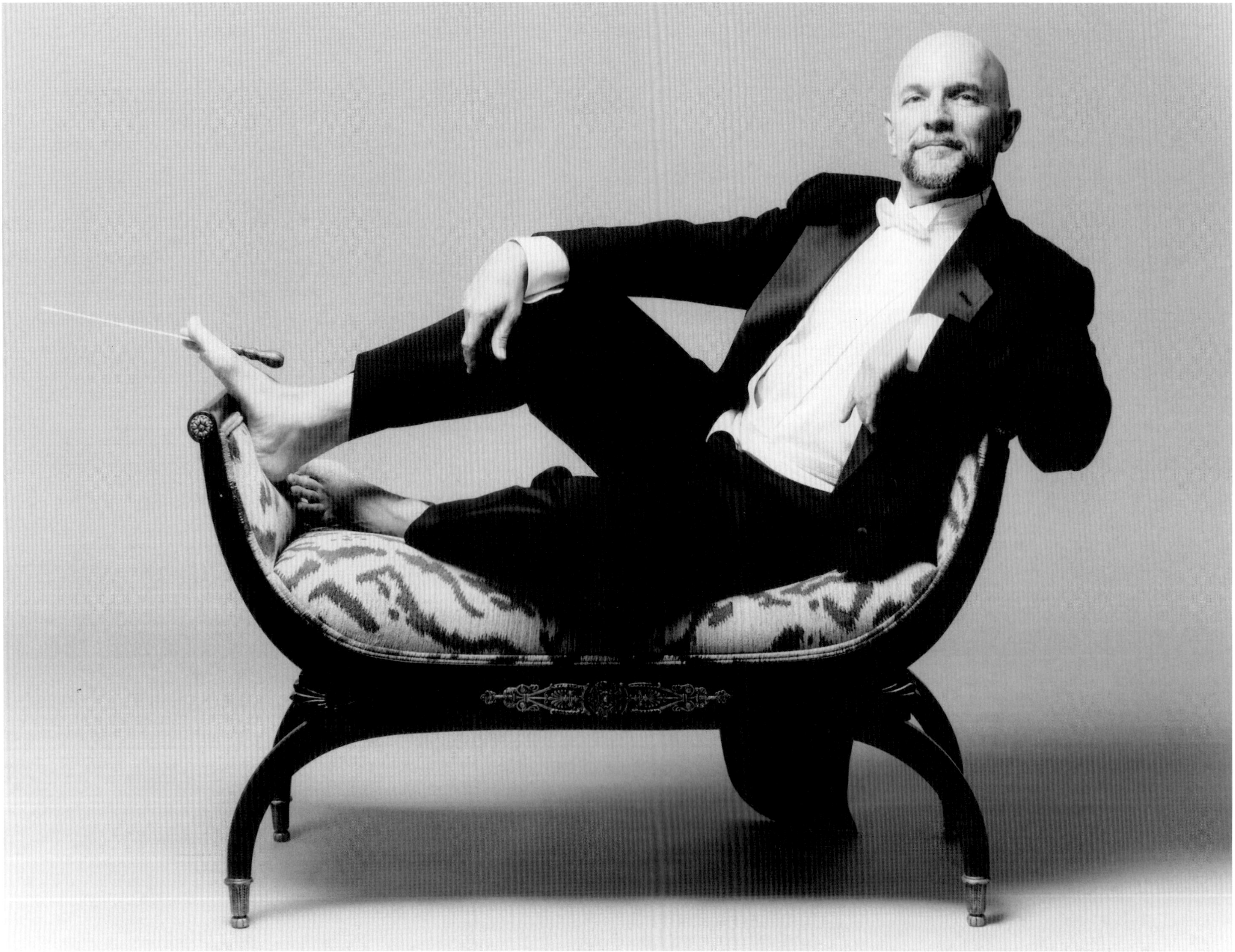

years ago he requested that the title be removed from his job description.) The busy office, with full-time employees David, Will, Kenn, Mark, Gretchen, Reed and Ella provide support. All know what Tim can do, and realize that they have to make room for the miraculous. Because no one knows where Tim's energies will take him, one has to be very quick to see how "groundless ground" becomes Tim's turf, and with no prior knowledge of his intention, it could well appear that he's just lunging about at the service of dreams and inspiration. In fact, he is an astute political tactician and the image of "groundless ground" (from "Sing for the Cure") is applied to him so often because observers see only the uncertainties ahead. But Tim is fearless, doesn't understand the meaning of no, and is dead certain he's on the right path even when he can't see where it leads.

Tim's life experience has been the perfect laboratory to develop his many talents. His Southern Baptist pedigree is flawless. He went to two Baptist colleges, taught in a third, and his father was the Vice President and his mother on the voice faculty of the largest Baptist seminary in the world. He had created the perfect Baptist life. He was a good husband to a beautiful, talented woman and the proud father of two beautiful children, a brilliant student, a beloved professor and music minister. Then he lost all of the above and moved into a Motel 6 two days after his painful and public coming out.

Destitute and in personal pain he came to the Turtle Creek Chorale (bankrupt itself at the time), stopped wrestling with his demons and took on the world. Whenever he wasn't engaging friends and enemies of the Chorale, he was still leading and showing others how to live without fear (David Jenkins, for example, professor and married father of triplets who was outed on the front page of the *Dallas Morning News*).

What Seelig teaches is something like "self-remembering": that we must know who we are, accept that we are enough, be true to our self-knowledge and not squander it by trying to fulfill fantasies that prevent us from living in reality. He wants his choristers to take the stage as people, not musicians, and sing from their hearts, not according to ideas that have been inculcated by "professionals." Rather than taking the stage to be someone else and escape painful developmental crises that have beset them as gay men, they should use the concentrated energies of performance to celebrate what they find in themselves. Rather than relying on their talent as a bag of tricks to win preferment over their fellows, they should open their very souls onstage and be one with these men.

Again and again these singers surpass themselves and afterward take home the lesson that Tim Seelig would have them learn: you are complete in yourself, you already have everything you need. Thus the frustrated teacher and churchman is able, finally, to transmit with love the knowledge that has guided him through shattering disillusionments to happiness and fulfillment in the "palace of truth."

Tickets to one of the first concerts for which admission was charged: June 24, 1980. ($2.50! What a bargain.)

I was a very little girl the last time I saw you. Still, I want you to know the impact you have had on my life....

I grew up at First Baptist in Houston. I remember you so vividly; how I looked forward to the Sundays you handled the special music. You were one of the people who taught me how to worship.

I remember when you left the church, too, and nobody would tell me why. I just caught words here and there. I never heard your name spoken again. And I remember the way I put it together as a little girl: there is something you can do that is so bad, it can make you disappear. It took years to overcome that perception, and my perception of God suffered for it too.

I am still a Christian. I believe, at the end of the day, it's still as close to Truth as we get. The bride is in rather shabby shape, and racism and sexism, along with homophobia, are cancers we haven't rooted out. Thank God for grace. I work with girls in my inner-city, black congregation who nurture a homophobia that, perhaps, is the only thing that makes them feel better about themselves. And I say: not here. Not with me. Being female and black is precious no matter what the world tells you, we will say the same thing about God's gay children. I seek to understand things in a biblical framework. But I tell them that my friends, and a man who taught me to worship have convinced me I'd rather err on the side of being too loving. In the end, I hope that God will find that more forgivable than the alternative.

peace
Shannon Wright

The future? Alone, but with his men humming in his head, Seelig will keep carrying the fight to the religious right, especially in Dallas, their stronghold. These people have "come out" against the Chorale, and cloaked in righteousness will oppose in particular attempts by the Chorale to change people's minds, so that audiences might hear the beauty in their singing, and not dismiss it as "temptation"; might acknowledge the Chorale's courage in confronting stone-throwers armed only with a song; might feel the love that emanates from the Chorale in performance, heart to heart, routing the certainties that nourish contempt, causing even hardheaded true believers to respond in kind as fellow human beings with moist eyes and the sense of a shared moment in whirling time.

Since the battle is being fought with love as a weapon—and emotions that flash like swords and words that buoy the spirits of the soldiers, inexhaustibly seeking a way inside closed minds to assert a common meaning—there are no spoils. The things destroyed—bigotry, ignorance, small-minded certainties of all kinds—have no value to anyone, and what arises to take their place—a tear, a tiny smile, a faint acknowledgment of shared humanity—is fragile and quickly wiped away…yet not forgotten. The Chorale's future is built of these small beginnings and souvenir moments. Money isn't piling up, but there is an accumulation when love is poured so often and prodigally.

Of course the chorale enjoys all the applause that rewards their love of art, but they are creating so much more: new opportunities for music-making and self-knowledge, for caring and sharing, reaching out and nurturing, building bridges and celebrating and laughing and leading. Most important of all, perhaps, they are creating love and warmth where there was only cool distrust. And where there was a fear of sharing time and space, a fear of something rubbing off or reaching too far inside—nameless, ugly fears—this man and that woman will at some point have felt that they have all the time in the world, and that the way they were touched within just now in this hall of song was tenderness itself…opening doors, opening so many doors that there's no surprise when the walls come down and they are no longer in a stuffy room full of people they don't know—they are among friends, taking their first steps inside a vast palace where they can…breathe!

Pictured is the first concert program introducing the new conductor to Dallas. Dr. Seelig arrived having amassed quite an impressive resume as a singer including European and American opera debuts as well as a Carnegie Hall solo recital. While he has not performed often with the TCC through the years, he has recorded two CD's: *Everything Possible* and *Two Worlds*.

122

What others have said:

"Known as a fine singer, he also slices a thick cut of ham."
>Fort Worth Star Telegram

"Dr. Seelig takes eclecticism to new heights."
>Grammy Magazine

"An accomplished chorale, under Dr. Timothy Seelig, the chorus is a disciplined group with a strong sound, considerable subtlety in dynamics and musical expression."
>USA Today

"The quality of Seelig's voice is lovely, fresh and supple. He is in command of all languages…is an expressive performer… capable of power."
>New York Times

"As fine a male chorus as I'll ever hope to hear."
>American Record Guide

"American Tim Seelig surprised the audience with vocal substance and great dramatic depth."
>Salzburger Nachrichten (Austria)

From top to bottom:

Dr. John and Virginia Seelig; Retreat fun; Tim and Craig – a dynamic working duo for 10 years.

(top left) In 1996, Tim was chosen as a community hero invited to carry the Olympic torch on its way through Dallas. He has not run since.

(bottom left) Dr. Seelig appearing with former First Lady Betty Ford. Graduation Day at the clinic?

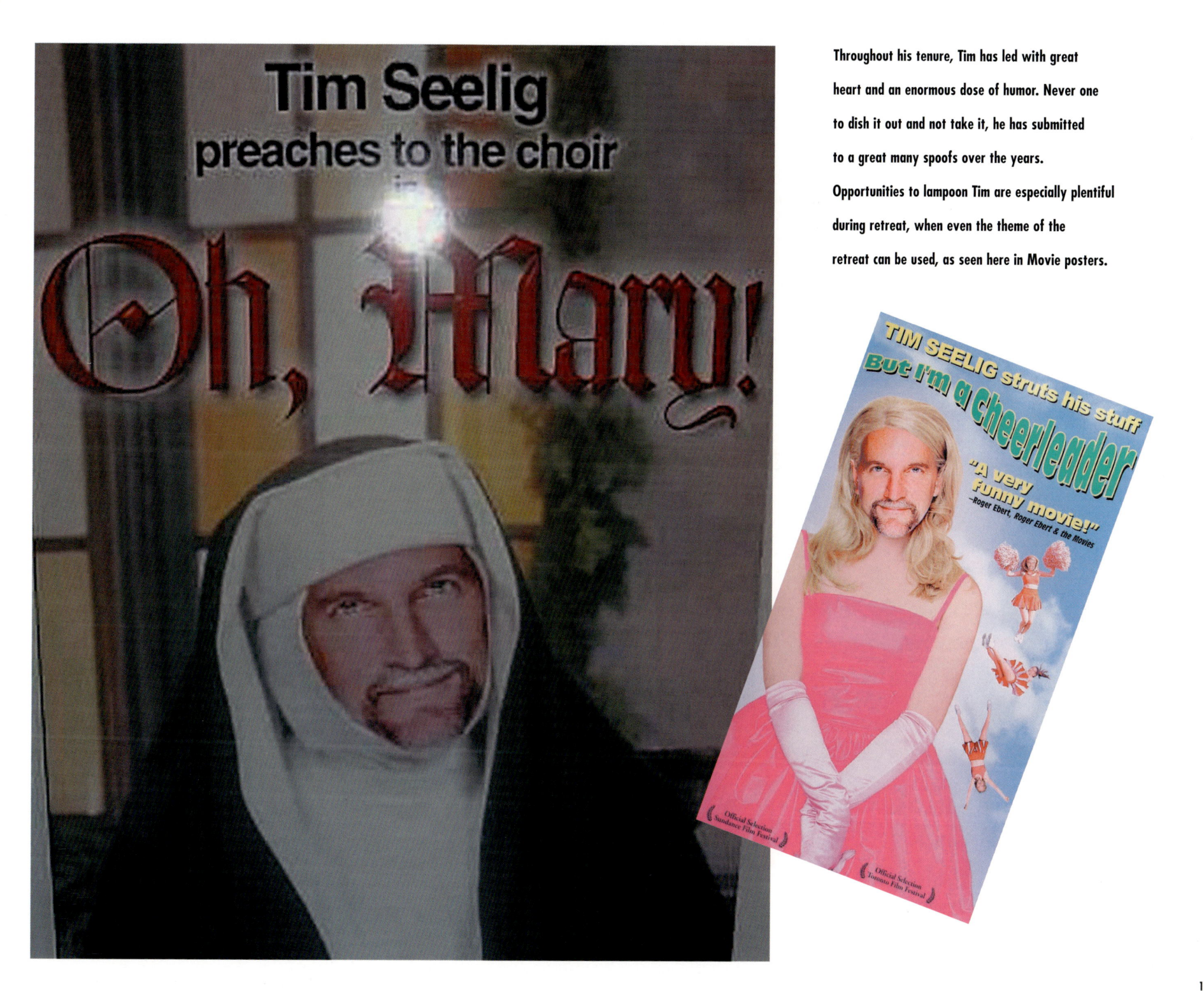

Tim Seelig preaches to the choir in Oh, Mary!

TIM SEELIG struts his stuff But I'm a Cheerleader
"A very funny movie!"
—Roger Ebert, Roger Ebert & the Movies

Official Selection Sundance Film Festival
Official Selection Toronto Film Festival

Throughout his tenure, Tim has led with great heart and an enormous dose of humor. Never one to dish it out and not take it, he has submitted to a great many spoofs over the years. Opportunities to lampoon Tim are especially plentiful during retreat, when even the theme of the retreat can be used, as seen here in Movie posters.

The men of Turtle Creek Chorale are joined by children of the Dallas ISD and the UTD/Callier Center for Communication Disorders on stage at the Meyerson Symphony Center, signing *Silent Night*. The 2003 Holiday concert, *Signs of Joy*, was broadcast on WFAA Channel 8 and sponsored by Verizon.

THE STERLING CIRCLE DONORS

Rick Aishman and Tom Phipps
Peter Anderson and David Metoyer, Jr.
G. William Armstrong, Jr.
Jeffrey J. Baker and Antonio Guzman
Ralph and Jo Blackburn
Tim and J. Pat Blanchard-Modisette
Tab Boyles
Dr. David Brand and George Anderson
David Breith and Zan Moore
Jeff Bright and Steve Gass
Dr. Barry J. Bryan
Rick Burns
T. Michael Chandler and Dennis Centorbi
Scott Davidson
James B. Evans
Robert R. Forner and Erin Thorkildsen
Lee and Susan Gammill
Steve Goetz and Jay DeMuynck
Keith Griffin
J.B. Holman
Ralph and Nicole Isenberg
George R. 'Jake' Jacobs
Bruce W. Jaster
Paul Kalasci III
Will Kolb and Gary Bellomy
Jim Knox
Jim Kondysar and Joey Miertschin
Dean Lester

Tom Malin
Dawn Meifert
Kathy Messina and Gary W. Goodwin
David Mitchell and David Elliott
Doug Mitchell and Ed Calcote
Ken Morris and Kevin McDaniel
Fred Owen
Kert Platner
Steven Pounders M.D. and James O'Reilly
W.L. Prather
Noel David Pullam and Darryl Clement
Joseph Rattan
James M. Rawson
Mike Renquist and Georjean Blanton
Louis Schneider and John D. Johnson
Timothy Seelig and Shawn Northcutt
Peter Sehnert and A.G. Black
Mark Arthur Shekter
Robert Steele
J. Christopher Stinnett
Skip and Mary M. Trimble
Robert Trost, Earl Whiteoak and Richard Rabb
D. Hal Unwin
Christopher J. Vesy and Alan E. Roller
John K. Watzling
Donna E. Wilson
Roger D. and Elizabeth L. Williams
Betty Youngman

THE STERLING CIRCLE
A Year of Investment… …A Lifetime of Returns

TURTLE CREEK CHORALE
The Power of Harmony

Imagine a world filled with music where people focused on harmony rather than their differences. What a truly magnificent dream. Two lone gentleman dared to imagine and twenty five years later their dream continues to grow and prosper. Throughout the years, the Turtle Creek Chorale has nurtured a very special relationship with a wonderful group of individuals; our donors. These giving and selfless people are an integral part of the power of harmony that the Chorale members so beautifully express in song.

Individual donors understand that ticket sales alone only cover half the expense of a concert. Patrons enable us to perform in such a glorious venue as the Morton H. Meyerson Symphony Center. They support the Chorale's continuing effort to provide free concert tickets to youth, senior citizens and persons living with AIDS. They uplift the Chorale as we bridge-build around the world through the power of music.

Finally, without our donors, the Turtle Creek Chorale could no longer continue to dream in new directions and plan for the future. Our individual donors have given so much and yet here, we thank those that have taken the extra step of joining the 25th Anniversary Sterling Circle. Each of these donors has pledged additional funds above and beyond their usual contributions insuring that the Turtle Creek Chorale will shine for the next twenty five years.

Our most heartfelt thanks.

Tim Seelig
Artistic Director

Will Kolb
Director of Development

Avenue Publishers, Inc.

4038 Lemmon Avenue

Dallas, Texas   75219

214-521-8600

www.avenuepublishers.com

TURTLE CREEK CHORALE
1980 ▶◀ 2005
25 YEARS OF HARMONY

Turtle Creek Chorale

Sammons Center for the Arts

P.O. Box 190137

Dallas, Texas   75219-0137

214-526-3214

fax   214-528-0673

www.turtlecreek.org

Dr. Timothy Seelig, *Artistic Director*

David L. Mitchell, *Managing Director*

Will Kolb, *Director of Development*

Jeff Putnam   *Writer and Publisher*

Mr. Putnam is the author of four published novels and has translated and co-written a number of biographical works. During his fourteen-year association with Baskerville Publishers he was responsible for the Great Voices series of opera biographies (issued, like this book, with compact discs), as well as books of literary criticism and literary history (he collaborated with author Ludmila Shtern to produce the memoir about Joseph Brodsky which appeared in October of this year). He has edited more than sixty books on many themes but has a special interest in vocal music, which he also performs (most recently last December as Colline in *La Bohème* for Maine Grand Opera). He lives in Dallas with his wife Dicia and son Samuel, and where another of his four children, Christian, is a software executive.

Avenue Publishers, Inc.   Dallas, Texas   214-521-8600   www.avenuepublishers.com

Joseph Rattan   *Design and Layout*

Mr. Rattan is a graduate of Texas Tech University and has been Design Director / Owner of Joseph Rattan Design in Dallas since 1988. His clients include Apple Computer, IBM, Coca Cola, Texas Instruments, International Paper, US West, Mary Kay Cosmetics among others. His work has been showcased in *Communication Arts*, *Print* and *Graphis* magazines; displayed by AIGA (American Institute of Graphic Arts), New York Art Directors Club and other exhibitions, and is included in the permanent collection of the United States Library of Congress. He taught Design Communications in the Department of Art at the University of North Texas. He resides in Dallas with his son, Christopher, who helped him create the illustrations in this book.

Joseph Rattan Design   Dallas, Texas   972-931-8044   www.josephrattandesign.com

Tom D. Land - Bryan Landsiedel - Lonnie Lane - Marie L. Lane - *Bob Lankow* - Paul R. LaPierre - Richard Lark - Brian Larrison - *Keith I. Lasley* - Chris LaVigne - Shawn M. Law - Rob Lawrence - David Lawson - Glyn LeBlanc - Alan Lee - Kirby Lee - Stuart R. Lee - Gene Lefler - Michael Leggett - James Lehman - Wai-Meng Leong - Jeffrey (Jeff) Lester - Bill Lewis - Jack Lewis - *Jeff Lewis* - K. Alan Lewis - Timothy Lewis - William (Bill) Lewis - Rocky L. Libich - Roy Lierman - Joe Liggett - Norman Liggett - Michael-David Light - Chris Liles - Michael Linder - Michael Liner - Davis Lipper - Jim Liss - Thomas Lloyd - Boyd - Michael Locke - Mark London - Kim Long-Groze - Mark Lonsway - Kevin Lord - Gary Loucks - Donal Lovell - Steve Lovett - *Norman Lowery* - Mitchell E. Lowther - Robert Lowther - Albert Lujan - Les Lujan - Chris Luna - Michael Lunce - David Lundy - Jim Luther - Chris Lyles - Robert L. Lynch, Jr. - Danny Macdougall - Joseph (Joey) Macias - Forrest MacLain - Jerry Maddox - Ron Maddox - Neil Makin - Tom Malin - Don Mallison - Glenn Mallory - *Larry Malone* - Phil Malone - Michael Maples - Marc Marchioli - Arthur Markart II - Gordon Markley - Joe Marland - *Randy Marr* - Jane Marshall - *Mike Marshall* - Wade Marshall - Bert Martin - Kevin D. Martin - Benjamin Martinez - *Ralph Masek* - Chris Mason - David Mason - Rick Mason - Jerry N. Massie - Scott Mathews - Fred Mauk - Jack Maus - Matthew (Matt) Mayer - Tim McAdams - Gary McAfee - Jim McBride - Kenneth E. (Kenn) McBryde - Bill McCain - Patrick J. (Pat) McCann, Jr. - *Jim McCaslin* - Wayne McClellan - Bruce McClelland - David McClinton - Jimmy McClinton - Paul McClinton - *Michael A. McConnell* - Niki McCustion - Jason McDaniel - Mike McDonald - Janet McEwin - *Phillip McFarland* - George McGarry - Joseph McGrann - Mark McGrath - Tom McKee - Greg McKenna - William H. McKinney, III - *Ken McLemore* - Rand McLeroy - *Bill McMaster* - Mike McMillen - Charles McMullen - Tom McMurtry - Eddie McMurty - Robert W. McWilliams - Kent Mecklenberg - Don Meissner - *Fred Melaun* - Peter Mena - Jessie Mercado - Buddy Mercer - Martin Meredith - *Mike Merrifield* - Michael Messmer - Steven Meyer - Allen Michero - Joey Miertschin - Tom Milan - Barry Miles - Mark Miles - Arlen Miller - *Charley Miller* - David Glenn Miller - David L. Miller - James L. Miller - Mark Miller - T. J. Miller - Terry Miller - Cassandra Gayle Mims - Jack Mion - Daniel H. Miot - Benjamin M. Mitchell - David Mitchell - Doug Mitchell - Steven C. (Steve) Mitchell - Steven Mitchell - Steven R. Mitchell - Rodney Moffett - David Moldenhauer - Andrew Molina - Oscar Monsibais - Tim Montiero - Scott Montroy - Frederick (Fred) E. Moore - Jack L. Moore - Jay Moore - Michael Moore - Todd Moore - *Ismael Morales* - Jon Morehouse - Edwin S. Morgan - James (Rex) Morgan - Mrs. James M. (Lynn) Moroney, Jr. - Ken Morris - Jim Morrison - Duayne Moseley - Ewing (Sandy) Moseley - Kevin Mountford - Raymon D. Moy - Jeff Moyer - *Larry Mueller* - Cameron Muhic - Thom Mulkey - *Barry Mullen* - Michael Mullen - Charles Mullins - Brian Mumey - John Murphree - Brett Murphy - Christopher Murphy - Jay Murra - Mike Murray - Randy Murray - Peter Mutnan - Rik Muzychenko - Paul Myers - Jeff Myrtle - *Kent Naasz* - Mark H. Nagel - Darrell Nakagawa - *Jim Nash* - Jerome Nave - Ken Naylor - Jeff Neal - Gene Nelson - Richard (Ric) Nelson - Joyce Nelson-Murphy - Clay Newlin - Terry Newsom - Alan Nguyen - Troy Nichelson - Glen Nichols - Rob Nichols - Ron Nichols - Jack Nightingale - Teresa Nix - Justin Normand - Shawn Northcutt - Jim Norwood - Eddie Nunns - *Mark O'Dell* - Daniel (Dan) Oakes - Shannon Oakes - Daniel Oberlender - Keith Odums - *Rick Oechsle* - Darrell Oldham - Bill Olds - Renee Olds - Brad Olesen - Drea Olson - *Gary Olson* - Miles Olson Robert Orndorff - Rick Ornelas - Kevin Orr - Tom Osborne - *Gary Osbourne* - Rusty Ouder - Fred Owen - Mark Elwyn Owen - Kevin Oyenik - David Ozebeck - Joe Pacetti - *Delman Painter* - Scott Palermo - Ernest Pardo - *Charles Pardue* - Jed A Pare, D.D. - Dana Parigo - *James (Jimmy) Parker* - Mark Turner Parker - Thad Parkes - Richard Parkman - Allen Parks - Lonnie Parks - Sandy Parks - Jeannie Parrent - Stan Paschal - John Pashley - M.J. Pashley - Steve Patterson - David Patton - James (Rex) Patton - Mike Paulus - Larry Pease - Bob Peck - Joao Meiredes Pedrosa-Neto - Dick Peeples - John Pelletti - Aryel Pena - Pete Pena - Joel Perkins - Larry Permenter - Michael (Mike) Peters - Bill Peterson - Timothy Peterson - Jack Pettit - Ron Petty - Chinh Duc Pham - Barry Phillips - Chris Pickett - *Dennis Plemmons* - David Ploof - Greg Poduska - Philip Poff - Fred Poggemeyer - Zach Pohl - Roger J. Poindexter, Jr. - Rudy Pollan - Warren (Curt) Porter - Michael Postal - Clayton Powell - Gary Powell - James Powell Kenneth Prentice - Rusty Prentice - Charles W. Price - Stephen W. Price - Joe Prieto - Matt Proffitt - Gary Prophett - David Pucek - Michael Pugh - Bill Pullen - Tom Pumphrey - Steve Punches - Dave Pursell - *Kris Rabonza* - Roger Radant - *David Rahencamp* - Michael Scott Raines - Hayley Rambo - Gabriel Ramirez - Louis Ramirez - Todd Ramsey - Chris Raney - Joseph Rattan - Bill Rauscher - Jamie Rawson - Danny W. Ray - Randall G. Ray - *Ricky Raymond* - Thomas Read - Franklin Reed - Julian V.C. Reed - Jimmy Renick - Scott Renno - Mike Renquist - Alan Reynolds - *Randall E. Rhea* - *Benjamin H. (Sandy) Rhodes* - Joe Rhyne - Mack Richard - David Richardson - *Leasel Richardson* - Paul W. Richey - Russ Rieger - *Roger Riels* - Gary Rifkin - Jamie Rifkin - David W. Riley - Ellen Ritscher - *Don Ritz* - Guadalupe (Lupe) Rivera, Jr. - *Richard Roberts* - Christopher G. Robertson - Wes Robertson - Craig Robinson - David Robison - *Edwin Rodriguez* - Orlando Rodriguez - David Rogers - James Romanoff - Jarrod James Romitti - Robert Rose - David Rosenlieb - David Ross - Jim Ross

- *Frank Rossiter* - Chuck Roundtree - *Keith Rowe* - Robert Rowell - David Rowland - Gary Rubenstein - *Mark C. Rucker* - Benny Ruiz, II - Shane Runyan - Gary Ruska - Jason Russell - Eric Ryan - Ami Sadeh - Leo Sadovy - Robert Salina - Tony Sare - *Art Saucedo* - Jeff Sauers - Raun Savage - Todd Savell - Brent Sawyer - Paul Scarbro - Brent Schafer - Harry E Scher - John Schertz - Edward Schiller - Don Schmidt - Karen Schnute - Larry Schoon - Val Schreiber - *Gene Schroeder* - Steve Schuller - Duane Schulund - Mark Schuttler - Eric Schwartz - Jon Schweikhard - Cleveland Scott, Jr. - Gretchen Scribner - *Matthew P. Seckman* - Dr. Timothy Seelig - Darrell Seidler - Christopher Seitz - Michael Serrecchia - *Steve Seufert* - Paul Seymour - Ray D. Shackleford - Rick Shackleford - Douglas Shaffer - John Share - Gerald Sharp - Cliff Sharpless - Michael Sharrett - Wayne Shaw - Victor Shea - Edward Sheen - Eric Shellhorn - Jim Shelton - Daniel L. Shipman - David Shipp - *Dan R. Shirley* - Kevin Shook - John S. Shore - Lee Shrum - Daniel Shtarkman - Randy Shull - James L. Sides - Patrick Sifuentes - David J. Silva - Bill Sime - Trace Simmons - John Sims - Robert Lamar Sims - Cecil Sinclair - *Joe Singer* - Brian Skinner - Pat Skinner - B. J. Smith - Billy Smith - Evan Randall Smith - Jim Smith - Mark Smith - *Roy Smith* - Scott Smith - Terry Smith Thomas Smith - Ed Smolen - Michael Smotherman - Jason Snedegar - Daryl Snyder - Joe Snyder - Mickey Snyder - John H. Solis - Mark Soward - Ben Sowders - David Spangler - James Spann - Keith Spargo - *Paul Spear* - Bill Spelman - Antoine Spencer - *Sid Spencer* - Harold Spiegel - James Spivey - Kevin Spivey - Steven Spradlin - Brian Spraggins - *Larry Spry* - Kevin St. Armant - Charles St. John - *Jim Stahlecker* - M. Bryan Stanley - Paul Starr - Randy Startz - Robert Steele - Frank Stegall - Andy Steingasser - *Michael Stephani* - *Bob Stephens* - Michael B. Stephens - Rodney Stephens - David B. Sterling - Thomas Sterns - Linda Stevens - Michael Stevens - David Stevenson - Ken Stewart - Robb Stewart - Samuel Stiles - *Rick Stillwell* - J. Christopher Stinnett - Robert Stinnett - Terry Stone - Gail Stoneking - Scott Stout - *Len Stoutt* - *Jeff Strachen* - David thor Straten-Mohr - Byron Strickland - Denise Stuart - Stacey Sturdivant - Keith Sublett - Michael D. Sullivan - *Bob (Ed) Sundstrom* - Eric Sundstrom - *Jeff Surber* - Ken Surley - Jason D. Swan - Chuck Sweatt - Clinton Talbert - Scott Talbert - Kyle Talkington - Robert Talley - Jim Tanselle - Jeffery Tarkington - *David Tate* - Curtis Tatro - Neil Taylor - Wayne Taylor - Timothy Teague - *Bob Teel* - Jeannette Teel - Stephen Teel - *Larry Teems* - Jerry A. Tennison - Randy Terrell - Thomas F. Thacker - Fred Theobald - James Thomas - *John Thomas* - Richard Thomas - Rod Thomas - Ronnie Thomas - Steven Thomas - Timothy Thomas - Dennis Thompson - Doug Thompson - Maurice Thompson - Rodney L. Thompson - Todd Thompson - Jimmy Thornton - Jim Tilley - Thomas Timbol - Anthony Todd - Bryan Tomes - Michael Toole - *Clinton Trammell* - Curtis Trammell - Anthony C. Trang - Irene Travis - Will Trice - Mark Trimble - Dain Trosper - Cary Trujillo - Tony Tucci - *Barry Tucker* - *Buzz Tucker* - Davey Turner - Lyndon Turner - Terry Turner - Jerry Tyler - *John Lee Tyler* - Allen Tyler-Shaw - Peggy Underwood - Jeff Updike - Paul Valdez - Andre Valk - *Jay Van Ness* - Loren Vandagriff - Shelley Vandergrift - *Bill Vanderlind* - Mark Vangeison - Will Varner - Robert Vaticalos - Randall Vaughn - Chris Vesy - Greg Vick - Victor Vidal - Mark Villalpando - David Villarreal - Jacob Villarreal - Victor Villegas - *Bobby Gene Vinson* - Shawn Wade - *Richard Waidelich* - Michael Waite - Jody Walden - David Walker - Edwin Walker - Jason Walker - John Walker - Reggie Walker - Rick Walker - Keith Wall - Brian Walsh - Paul M. Walters, II - Sterling Walton - Ed Ward - Kevin Washington - B. Kip Watkins - Durward A Watson -Kevin R. Watson - William Waybourn - Brian Weart - Albert Webb - Gary Webb - Rick Webb - Daniel Weber - *Joan Wedlake* - Kjersti Weingardt - Kip Welch - Jerry L. Wellman - Trace Wendell - Bill J. West - Brian West - *Joel West* - Michael West - Rev. Carol W. West - Bruce Westbrook - John Westfield - Gregory Westmoreland - Jonathan Wheat Jon Wheaton - Timothy Wheeler -Gary W. White - Jimmy White - Randy White - Michael Whiteside - Mark Whitfield - Frank Whitington - Norman Whitlock - Justin Whitney - Phillip Wier - Lance Wiesmann - *Mark Wiginton* - Paul Wignall - James A. Wilcox, III - Alberta Wilkerson - Del Wilkinson - Kay Wilkinson - *Wayne Wilkinson* - Brian E. Willette - Dave Williams - Gary Williams - J. T. Williams - Jay Williams - Jim Williams - Jonathan Williams - Paul Williams - Ross Williams - Shannon Williams - Ted Williamson - Burnell Willis - Cindy Wilson - David Ray Wilson - David Wilson - *Rodger Mark Wilson* - Jeff Wincek - *Steve Windsor* - William Wingo - Robert Winn - Ray Witherspoon - Jerry Wolfe - Brent Wood - Roy Wood - Thomas Wood - Wayne Wooderson - Cody Woodfin - Dorian Woodruff - J. Weston Woods - Stephen Worley - Mark Wright - Michael Wyatt - *Bill Yates* - Richard M. York, Jr. - *Dick Young* - Ed Young - Michael Young - Robert S. Young - Gary N. Youngblood - Timm Zitz - T. J. Zottola, Jr. (*as of August 1, 2004*)